Morphing On Your PC

David K. Mason

Waite Group Press™
Corte Madera, California

Publisher • *Mitchell Waite*
Editorial Director • *Scott Calamar*
Managing Editor • *John Crudo*
Production Director • *Julianne Ososke*
Content Editor • *Harry Henderson*
Technical Reviewer • *John Blanchard*
Design • *Cecile Kaufman*
Producton • *Sestina Quarequio*
Cover Design • *Ted Mader*

Published by Waite Group Press™, 200 Tamal Plaza, Corte Madera, CA 94925.

Waite Group Press is distributed to bookstores and book wholesalers by Publishers Group West, Box 8843, Emeryville, CA 94662, 1-800-788-3123 (in California 1-510-658-3453).

Printed in the United States of America
94 95 96 • 10 9 8 7 6 5 4 3 2 1

Library of Congress Cataloging in Publication Data
Mason, David (David Keith), 1964-
      Morphing on your PC / David K. Mason.
          p.   cm.
    Includes index
    ISBN: 1-878739-53-0: $29.95
    1. Computer Graphics.   2. Metamorphosis.
T385.M374 1993
006.6--dc20

93-34428
CIP

DEDICATION

To my sister, Mary Ellen Dolmat, her husband George, and their spectacular kids Danny, Sarah, David, and Rebekah.

To my brother, Gerard Mason, his wife Donna, and their wonderful daughter Courtney.

To my dear friends Jerry, Lin, and Brick Maloney, who are like another family to me.

ACKNOWLEDGMENTS

I owe a lot to Doug Smythe, for his pioneering work in morphing at Industrial Light and Magic, and to George Wolberg, for his fantastic book about morphing and other warping effects, *Digital Image Warping*. This book (and the DMorf program) couldn't exist without their work.

I also want to thank Mitch Waite, for giving me the chance to write this book; John Crudo, expert managing editor, for keeping this project moving; Julianne Ososke and her production crew, for turning the manuscript into a real book; Harry Henderson, whose skill, insight, and editing greatly improved the book; and John Blanchard for his efficient technical review.

More thanks go to Trilobyte, for allowing me to use their program Play with this book.

Thanks also to the gang of morphing, graphics, and animation fanatics on CompuServe's GRAPHDEV forum and on The Graphics Alternative BBS (Eric Kachelhofer, Lutz Kretzschmar, Ken Condal, Jeff Bowermaster, Dan Farmer, Alexander Enzmann, Eric Deren, and many more) for catching all of those bugs and coming up with all of those great ideas.

Thanks to the Universe gang (Pendragon, LOPE, Bro, Leoj, Braniac, Futura, Gronk, and Phid) for inspiration and for being truly warped individuals.

ABOUT THE AUTHOR

David K. Mason

Dave Mason became obsessed with computer graphics (of a sort) as a teenager, fiddling away on a black-and-white TRS-80 Model I. Now an after-hours 3-D rendering and animation freak, he's the author of DTA, DMorf, and a few other computer animation utilities. In real life, he works at a major software house, writing programs which, alas, have absolutely nothing whatsoever to do with making movies. He received a degree in English at Northeastern University. Dave co-authored *Making Movies on Your PC* (Waite Group Press, 1993) with Alexander Enzmann.

Dear Reader

What is a book? Is it perpetually fated to be inky words on a paper page? Or can a book simply be something that inspires—feeding your head with ideas and creativity regardless of the medium? The latter, I believe. That's why I'm always pushing our books to a higher plane; using new technology to reinvent the medium.

I wrote my first book in 1973, *Projects in Sights, Sounds, and Sensations*. I like to think of it as our first multimedia book. In the years since then, I've learned that people want to experience information, not just passively absorb it—they want interactive MTV in a book. With this in mind, I started my own publishing company and published *Master C*, a book/disk package that turned the PC into a C language instructor. Then we branched out to computer graphics with *Fractal Creations*, which included a color poster, 3-D glasses, and a totally rad fractal generator. Ever since, we've included disks and other goodies with most of our books. In addition to software, *Virtual Reality Creations* is bundled with 3-D Fresnel viewing goggles, and *Walkthroughs & Flybys CD* comes with a multimedia CD-ROM. We've made complex multimedia accessible for any PC user with *Ray Tracing Creations, Multimedia Creations, Making Movies on Your PC, Image Lab*, and three books on Fractals.

The Waite Group continues to publish innovative multimedia books on cutting-edge topics, and of course the programming books that make up our heritage. Being a programmer myself, I appreciate clear guidance through a tricky OS, so our books come bundled with disks and CDs loaded with code, utilities, and custom controls.

By the end of 1994, The Waite Group will have published over 135 books. Our next step is to develop a new type of book, an interactive, multimedia experience involving the reader on many levels.

With this new book, you'll be trained by a computer-based instructor with infinite patience, run a simulation to visualize the topic, play a game that shows you different aspects of the subject, interact with others on-line, and have instant access to a large database on the subject. For traditionalists, there will be a full-color, paper-based book.

In the meantime, they've wired the White House for hi-tech; the information super highway has been proposed; and computers, communication, entertainment, and information are becoming inseparable. To travel in this Digital Age you'll need guidebooks. The Waite Group offers such guidance for the most important software—your mind.

We hope you enjoy this book. For a color catalog, just fill out and send in the Reader Report Card at the back of the book. You can reach me on CIS as 75146,3515, MCI mail as mwaite, and usenet as mitch@well.sf.ca.us.

Sincerely,

Mitchell Waite

Mitchell Waite
Publisher

Waite
Group
Press ™

Morphing on Your PC

PREFACE xi

INSTALLATION xiii

CHAPTER 1: INTRODUCTION 1

CHAPTER 2: DMORF TUTORIAL 17

CHAPTER 3: TRICKS AND TECHNIQUES 37

CHAPTER 4: TOOLS REFERENCE 67

CHAPTER 5: MORPHING PORTFOLIO 113

MORPHING CONTEST 161

INDEX 163

Contents

PREFACE xi

INSTALLATION xiii
    Hardware Required. xiii
    Installing the Files xiv
    Configuring Your Memory. xv
    Automatic Disk Compression. xvi
    Running in Microsoft Windows. xvi
    Running in OS/2 2.x xviii
    Presto Change-o xviii

CHAPTER 1: INTRODUCTION 1
    What is Morphing 3
        3-D Morphing Versus 2-D Morphing. 5
    The Fascination of Morphing 6
        Myths and Legends 7
    The Development of Morphing. 8
        Morphs in Movies 10
        Morphs in Television Programs. 11
        Morphs in Music Videos 11
        Morphs in Commercials and Advertisements. 13
    Other Applications and Possibilities 14
        Animation 15
    Get Ready to Explore. 15

CHAPTER 2: DMORF TUTORIAL 17

Step 1: Pick Two Pictures 20
Step 2: Start up DMorf 21
Step 3: Create the Control Mesh 22
Step 4: Test the Morph 29
Step 5: Refine the Mesh 31
Step 6: The Final Morph 34
Summary 36

CHAPTER 3: TRICKS AND TECHNIQUES 37

Sources 40
    Scan Them 40
    Video Digitizers 40
    Rendering 42
    Bulletin Boards and Online Services 44
    CD-ROMs 44
Faster Processing 45
Lighting 46
The Background Problem 47
    Creating Pictures with Transparency 48
    Adding Transparency to Preexisting Pictures .. 49
        Painting a Mask 49
    Compositing 56
"Just Warp" Effects 57
    Caricatures 57
    Moving Objects 60
Symmetric Morphs 61
Stringing Multiple Morphs Together 64
Output to Video 65
    The Way Pros Do It 65
    The Cheap Way 65
Summary 66

CHAPTER 4: TOOLS REFERENCE 67

DMorf 70
    Command-line Syntax 71
    The DMorf Screen 73
    The GUI Controls 74
        Buttons 74
        Check Boxes 74

Radio Buttons 74

Number Boxes 75

Text Boxes. 75

Menus on the Main Screen 75

The Max Screen 78

The Edit Screen 80

The Settings Dialog 82

The Screen Colors Dialog 85

The Pictures Dialog 86

The DMorf Mesh File Format. 88

DTA 90

Shareware Information 91

Preparation. 91

Creating a Simple Flic 92

Files That DTA Can Read 93

Command-line Switches 94

Output File Format (/F) 95

Output File Name (/O) 95

Resolution (/R#) 95

Speed (/S#). 96

Repeating Frame (/REP#) 97

Color Selection 98

Dithering. 99

Picture Scaling (/SC) 102

Picture Clipping (/CL) 104

Picture Placement (/ST) 104

Frame Averaging (/A# and /T#) . . . .

Multiple Layers (/L) . . . .

Chroma-Key (/CH, /CI#) . . . .

Skipping Frames (/C#, /K#, /I#) 107

Frame Expansion (/X#) 108

Ping Pong (/P) 108

3-D (/3D). 108

Creating Targa Files (/NC, /B#) 109

FLISPEED 109

Trilobyte Play 110

Running Play 110

Changing Speed 111

Looping. 111

Memory. 111

Changing Luminence 111

Summary. 112

CHAPTER 5: MORPHING PORTFOLIO 113

Danny and George.. 116
    Building the Danny and George Morph........................... 116
    Discussion 117
Pendragon and P.J... 118
    Building the Pendragon and P.J. Morph.......................... 119
    Discussion 119
Owl/Bear... 120
    Building the Owl/Bear Morph................................... 121
    Discussion 123
Danny and Sarah 123
    Building the Danny and Sarah Morph 124
    Discussion 125
Erosion 125
    Building the Erosion Morph 126
    Discussion 126
Dog 128
    Building the Dog Morph 128
    Discussion 129
Cars.. 130
    Building the Cars Morph....................................... 131
    Discussion 132
Dino-boy.. 133
    Building the Dino-boy Morph................................... 133
    Discussion 134
Roofs... 136
    Building the Roofs Morph...................................... 136
    Discussion 137
Flying 137
    Building the Flying Warp....................................... 139
    Discussion 140
Watch 141
    Building the Watch Morph 141
    Discussion 143
Planetary Evolution 143
    Building the Planet Morph 144
    Discussion 145
Genie in a Bottle.. 149
    Building the Genie Morph...................................... 149
    Discussion 150

Robot 153
    Building the Robot Morph 154
    Discussion 155
Summary. 159
The Fat Lady Sings. 160

MORPHING MAGIC CONTEST. 161

INDEX. 163

Preface

Image morphing is a lot like electronic alchemy. You start with one digital image, then transform it into something else. Using morphing techniques, you can perform magic that would even impress Merlin—make a genie pop out of a bottle, turn yourself into a howling werewolf, or create a universe from a cloud of dust.

You've no doubt seen computerized morphing as a special effect in advertising, TV, and movies, but this is no longer high-end technology. As the tools become increasingly available, it is appearing in traditional computer fields such as video games and multimedia presentations. In fact, morphing may be spreading to additional applications in the fields of medicine, criminology, and business.

Morphing on Your PC shows both new and experienced PC users how to take advantage of this latest and greatest image-processing technique. Through hands-on examples and instruction, you learn how to use the bundled programs to create cutting-edge computer graphics on your own computer.

The five chapters in this book introduce you to the concepts behind the technology, then show you how to quickly generate your own morphs. This complete package makes it easier than you might think to produce dazzling special effect imagery.

◆ **Chapter 1, Introduction** covers the background of morphing. You'll find out what actually defines morphing, learn how to distinguish between image and object morphing, and review the development of this innovative technology.

◆ **Chapter 2, DMorf Tutorial** walks you through the process of building a simple morph animation. You'll jump right in and learn the six steps of basic morphing by creating a morph of your own. Discover how to select, load, and transform images through practical application.

◈ **Chapter 3, Tricks and Techniques** presents more advanced morphing techniques. Once you've learned how to construct a basic morph, you'll want to learn some of the fancier tweaks and tricks the pros use. Find out how to make your special effects more dazzling with the use of warping, lighting, masking, and other means.

◈ **Chapter 4, Tools Reference** focuses on the four shareware programs that accompany the book. You will be able to take full advantage of the features provided by these utilities after learning about their specific controls, parameters, and syntax. Once you've mastered the tools, you will have more options and control when crafting your morphs.

◈ **Chapter 5, Morphing Portfolio** includes 14 finished morph animations. Complete descriptions and details allow you to reproduce them. The disk includes the morphs and the images so you'll have plenty of ideas and pictures to work with. You can experiment with the provided examples or use them for inspiration or as a starting point for your own morph creations.

Learn how to create image magic on your own computer. Take your high-tech magician's wand in hand and start *Morphing on Your PC!*

Installation

This book includes several shareware programs that help you create morphed animations:

◆ DMorf—A 2-D image morphing program. It lets you design and build multiple-image transformations between two images, and to warp images in almost any manner you want.

◆ DTA—A versatile image format conversion program. We will mostly use it for assembling sequences of frames into flic files. It also allows you to build GIF-format still pictures from DMorf's output.

◆ Trilobyte Play—This program plays the flic files that you build with DTA on your VGA or SVGA display. It also supports flics built with Autodesk's Animator Pro and 3-D Studio, and many other programs.

HARDWARE REQUIRED

Table 1 shows several different hardware configurations: the absolute minimum to run the software; then the minimum system required to actually get much accomplished in your lifetime; and finally, a system that will let you get the most out of the software.

Two versions of the DMorf program are provided: DMORF.EXE, for systems with math coprocessors, and DMORFNC.EXE, for systems with no coprocessor. While either version will work whether you've got a coprocessor or not, you'll lose a lot of performance by using the wrong version; especially

Hardware	Minimum	Efficienct	Ideal
Processor	80286	80386SX or DX, or 80486SX	80486 DX2/66 or Pentium
RAM	2MB	4MB	16MB (You can have more, but Dmorf won't be able to use it.)
Hard disk	20MB	80MB	500MB
Video adapter	VGA	VESA SVGA, 640 x 480 x 256	Accelerated VESA SVGA, 1024 x 768 x 256
Additional	Microsoft-compatible mouse	Mouse, math coprocessor, grayscale hand scanner	Mouse, color flatbed scanner. No coprocessor needed because it's built it's into the processor chip

Table 1

if you run the regular DMORF.EXE on a machine without a coprocessor. Table 2 displays the amount of time that it took each of the two programs to process a one-frame morph between two 320 x 200-pixel images on three different machines.

If you don't have a floating-point unit, you should delete the file DMORF.EXE and replace it with DMORFNC.EXE. Do this by typing:

```
del dmorf.exe
rename dmorfnc.exe dmorf.exe
```

INSTALLING THE FILES

To install the morphing tools and example files, insert the first bundled disk in your 3.5-inch floppy disk drive. At the DOS prompt type:

Wait! If your drive is drive B, then use "b:" instead of "a:" in the following command. If you want these files installed on a drive other than drive C, then use it instead of "c:".

```
a:install a: c:
```

When this batch program is done, remove the disk and insert the second floppy disk. Again, type:

```
a:install a: c:
```

System	DMORF.EXE	DMORFNC.EXE
80486 DX2-50, built-in math coprocessor	36 sec.	1 min., 28 sec.
80486 DX-33, built-in math coprocessor	44 sec.	1 min., 58 sec.
80386 DX-25, no math coprocessor	49 min., 34 sec.	4 min., 55 sec.

Table 2

When the batch installation program is done, the morphing tools and their document files will be in a directory called MORPHING\TOOLS. Example files will be in other subdirectories beneath MORPHING. Example files for Chapter 2 will be in MORPHING\CHAP2, Chapter 3 examples will be in MORPHING\CHAP3, and so on.

You should edit your AUTOEXEC.BAT file so that the directory with the MORPHING\TOOLS utilities is in your PATH statement. If you told the installation program to put the files on the C drive, your PATH statement should look something like this:

```
PATH C:\;C:\DOS;C:\WINDOWS;C:\MORPHING\TOOLS
```

The directories at the beginning of the line will vary from system to system. Note that the new path won't take effect until your computer has been restarted.

CONFIGURING YOUR MEMORY

DTA and DMorf require extra memory to be allocated as extended (XMS) memory, while Play requires expanded (EMS) memory in order to load large animation files. Fortunately, most modern memory-management software (QEMM-386, 386^{MAX}, and even DOS 6's HIMEM.SYS and EMM386.EXE) allows you to allocate your memory as both types of memory simultaneously.

If you're using MS-DOS 6 and want to install HIMEM and EMM386 so that the programs included with this book can get all the memory that they need, use MS-DOS's MEMMAKER utility to configure your machine. See the MS-DOS documentation for more details.

If you're using MS-DOS 5 or earlier, it's probably more trouble than it's worth to run both HIMEM and EMM386. The two memory managers don't share a common pool of memory, so whatever you claim for expanded memory you can't use for extended memory. Unless you've got so much memory in your system that you can afford to spread it around, you'd be better off either using a separate memory management system like those listed above, or upgrading to MS-DOS 6.

AUTOMATIC DISK COMPRESSION

All of the programs included with this book work just fine with hard drives compressed by automatic disk compression programs like Stacker and SuperStor. Because of the large number and size of many picture files you'll be creating when you morph, you may find that you *need* to run such a compressor.

If you use such a compression program, make sure that you back up your important files regularly. This would be good advice even if you don't compress your disk, but it's even more important if you do. Some people use them without ever encountering a glitch, but there are plenty of horror stories too.

RUNNING IN MICROSOFT WINDOWS

All of the programs included with this book can be run fine inside a DOS window in Microsoft Windows 3.1 *if* you modify the DOSPRMPT.PIF configuration file properly. No matter how much memory is available to Windows, the programs won't be able to access it unless you fix the PIF, and they will probably run out of memory. Follow these steps:

1. In the Windows Program Manager, click on the PIFEDIT icon (unless you moved it elsewhere, you'll find it in the Main folder).

2. In the PIF Editor program, pull down the File menu and click on the Open button.

3. In the Open dialog's File Name list box, select DOSPRMPT.PIF, and then click on the OK button. At this point, the PIF Editor window should look like Figure 1.

4. Click on the number box labeled 'KB Limit' at the end of the line that begins "EMS Memory," and change the default of 1024 to a comfortably higher number like 8000.

5. Do the same with the XMS Memory KB Limit number box.

6. While you're in the PIF Editor, make sure that Display Usage is set to Full Screen, not Windowed.

7. In the File menu, click on the Exit command. When a dialog box asks whether it's okay to save the current changes, click on the Yes button.

DTA will run in either a full-screen or a windowed DOS box, but DMorf and Play require full screen. If you run DMorf or Play in a Super VGA graphics mode, you should avoid changing to other tasks while the program runs. Windows will not be able to reset the graphics mode properly when you switch back, and you'll be stuck with a screen full of garbage. If you forget and do switch sessions with (ALT)-(TAB) while running DMorf, don't worry too much. DMorf will continue to run properly except for the nonsense on the screen. At any of the menus, you can press (ALT)-(R) to make DMorf redraw the screen. If you're running a standard VGA mode (640 x 480 in 16 colors for DMorf, or 320 x 200 in 256 colors for Play), then you won't run into this problem at all.

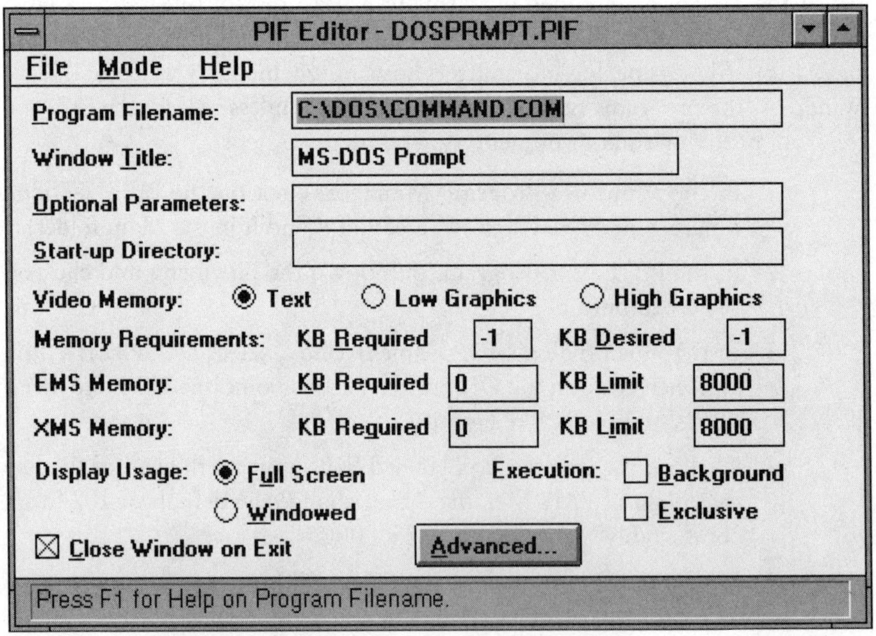

Figure 1 Editing DOSPRMPT.PIF with the PIF Editor

RUNNING IN OS/2 2.X

These programs also run just fine in an OS/2 "DOS Full Screen" window. Again, you'll have to configure the DOS session to assure that OS/2 allocates enough memory for the programs to work with. To configure the DOS window, follow these steps:

1. In the Command Prompts program group, click the right mouse button on the DOS Full Screen icon.

2. In the menu that pops up, click the left button on the little down-arrow next to the Open command, and then click on Settings.

3. When the Settings dialog pops up, click on the Session tab, and then on the DOS Settings button.

4. In the DOS Settings dialog, scroll the Setting: list box until the EMS_MEMORY_LIMIT setting is visible.

5. Click on EMS_MEMORY_LIMIT to select that setting, and then click on the number box below the Value: heading.

6. Type in a comfortably large number in the Value: box, like 4096 or 8000.

7. Scroll down the list box some more until XMS_MEMORY_LIMIT is visible, and change that number too.

8. Click on the Save button. OS/2 is now properly configured. Whenever you wish to run any of the morphing tools, just click on the DOS Full Screen icon to get at a DOS command line.

Unlike Windows, OS/2 has no problem restoring the screen after you switch between settings using (CTRL)-(ESC), regardless of the graphics mode you're using.

PRESTO CHANGE-O

You've installed the software on your hard disk, and are ready to run. Now get ready to take your high-tech magician's wand in hand and start creating your own stunning morph animations.

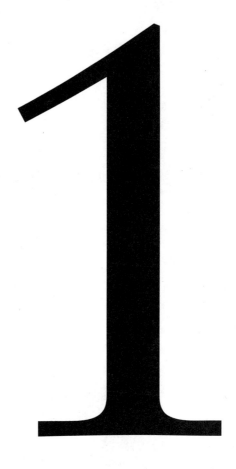

Introduction

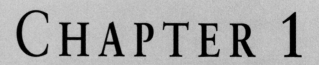

CHAPTER 1

Introduction

Go ahead, give yourself the body of Arnold Schwarzenegger without breaking a sweat. Turn iron into gold. Build a castle out of clouds. Change a full-grown man into a little boy. Thanks to an innovative computer technology called *morphing*, such transformations are no longer the exclusive domain of wizards, alchemists, gods, and plastic surgeons. They're a lot easier, too. While Merlin required huge spell books, numerous incantations, and ingredients like dragon spleens to accomplish such magic, morphing lets you produce similar results with a lot less hassle.

Morphing has literally changed the face of movies, TV, and music videos; it is already a standard special effect in entertainment and advertising. As this technology has developed, it has grown more accessible to other computer users; as a result, you no longer need a studio-sized budget to create superior special effects and image transformations. With the tools and techniques provided in this book, you can become a morphing wizard right in front of your own PC.

WHAT IS MORPHING?

Morphing is a computer-driven special effects technique that allows you to smoothly transform an image of one object into another. Although this electronic method is a relatively recent phenomenon, the idea of changing form, or *metamorphosis*, has been around since people first spun tales while huddling around a fire.

Warping Picture 1

Warping Picture 2

Blending the warped frames

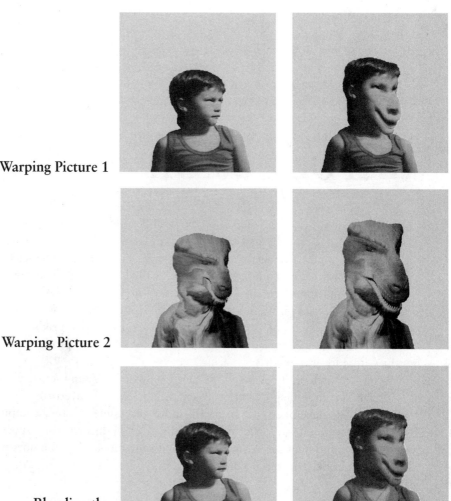

Figure 1-1 How morphing works

Starting with pictures of two images, a computer can incrementally warp the geometry of both pictures, melting one into another. The shape of the first object is fitted to the shape of the second object, and at the same time, one set of warped pictures fades to another. Figure 1-1 illustrates the process with pictures of Michael ("Brick") Maloney and the Boston Museum of Science's Tyrannosaurus Rex.

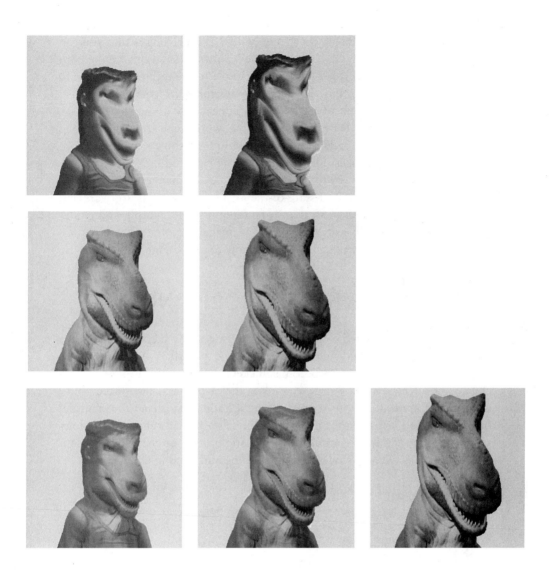

3-D Morphing Versus 2-D Morphing

There are two very different methods of creating morph effects. One, 3-D or *object* morphing, transforms one three-dimensional model of an object into another. The morphed models are then rendered into pictures. Using model building and rendering techniques allows for very realistic morphs of objects

that don't really exist. The main problem with 3-D morphing is that you can only use it if you've got models of what you want to morph; this can be both time-consuming and expensive. A classic example of the technique, shown in Figure 1-2, can be seen in the 1991 film *Terminator 2: Judgment Day,* when the evil terminator rises out of the floor to assume a human shape.

The second method, 2-D or image morphing, works by warping and fading between pictures that already exist. An example is shown in Figure 1-3. *Terminator 2: Judgment Day* also included many high-end 2-D effects. Close-up scenes in which the T-1000 terminator flawlessly changes into a human form are possible as a result of state-of-the-art image morphing software and techniques. With a lot less effort than is required to build, morph, and render 3-D models, you can still easily transform one image to another. The programs and lessons in this book will help you learn how to create simple 2-D morphs.

THE FASCINATION OF MORPHING

Why are people fascinated by shape changing? Certainly metamorphosis is a natural part of life. Disgusting furry bugs become butterflies. Adorable babies become spoiled children. Eggs become chickens. Milk turns into a horrifying chunky mess whenever you forget to look in the carton first. Two-faced politicians are different people in front of different audiences. It isn't that unusual for one thing to actually turn into something else. But morphing technology gives you a greater appreciation for the drastic process of change, because it allows you to see these changes taking place instantly and in living color.

Figure 1-2 A high-end object (3-D) morph from *Terminator 2: Judgment Day* (1991)

Figure 1-3 Using the tools in this in this book, you'll be able to create image (2-D) morphs, like this owl-bear combo

Morphing also provides the magical power to perform impossible feats, if only on a movie, computer, or television screen. You can use it to create strange new life-forms, renovate entire cities, make an ugly duckling turn into a swan, or turn any foolish mortal who dares to offend you into a toad. Let Merlin try to top that.

Myths and Legends

While the recent morphing special effects are innovative, the idea of a creature transforming into another shape is anything but new. The legends and myths of almost every culture, many tales of which originated even before the written word, include stories of shape-changing creatures and form-altering deities. A number of the Greek and Roman gods used shape changing to achieve their objectives. Zeus, for example, transformed himself into animals such as a bull, ram, and swan to prevent his wife Hera from discovering him while he seduced mortal women. A lesser god, Proteus, changed shape almost constantly, as he made himself into monsters, flames, floods, or pretty much anything at all. The Roman god Mercury, the patron of thieves, could alter his appearance so effectively he inspired the word *mercurial,* which means "changing in character."

Such tales are not confined exclusively to Greco-Roman culture. Native American legend tells of the mischievous trickster Coyote, who turned himself into a variety of animals to camouflage his practical jokes. Norse mythology has the wicked god Loki, who often transformed his shape to carry out his diabolical plots. Ancient Celtic lore, which heavily influenced the Arthurian legends, introduced the wizard Merlin as a shape shifter who could assume any form he chose. Forests throughout medieval Europe were believed to be the realm of werewolves and vampires—cursed men who, under certain influences, became hideous monsters. Even the fairy tales of Hans Christian Andersen, the Brothers Grimm, and others, included shape-changing themes. "The Frog Prince," "Beauty's Beast," "The Ugly Duckling," and "Pinocchio" (who was transformed from a puppet into a little boy after he finally got that nose morphing under control), all featured an awkward or beastly hero who eventually turned into a beautiful creature.

THE DEVELOPMENT OF MORPHING

Special effects experts tried for many years to create convincing transformations. Before Hollywood was able to embrace computer technology, such effects were tedious and difficult. In the 1931 movie *Dracula,* hand-drawn animation served to transform Bela Lugosi into a bat. In other motion pictures, like the 1941 film *The Wolf Man,* hours of makeup were responsible for the final morphing effect. Jack Pierce was the era's master makeup artist, the "morph" magician for *The Wolf Man.* Lon Chaney Jr. would be filmed many times in succession, each time wearing slightly different makeup. Much like shooting an animation film, each shot was filmed separately in sequential order, adding makeup effects in a gradual process. The filmmakers then created *dissolves* between each clip for a time-lapse photography effect. The horrifying end effect was the transformation into a werewolf right in front of a terrorized theater audience, shown in Figure 1-4

Without big budgets or the technical innovation of our age, most metamorphic effects were created using *misdirection,* the old trick that the magician uses to get you to watch the hand with the magic wand in it instead of the hand that's slipping a playing card out of his sleeve. In the 1958 movie *The Fly,* a scientist is transformed into a bug while hidden from the camera by his disintegration chamber. In the 1970s television series "Space: 1999," the camera would zoom into Maya's eye, and when it zoomed back out, she had transformed into another shape. Improved hydraulics in the 1980s allowed

Figure 1-4 Using simple camera tricks Lon Chaney, Jr. metamorphized from man to beast in *The Wolf Man* (1941)

films such as *Altered States* and *American Werewolf in London* to use inflatable bladders beneath an actor's facial makeup to create the illusion of a man devolving into a primitive Neanderthal or a blood-thirsty canine.

In 1988, Industrial Light and Magic (ILM) coined the term "morph" when creating the software to support a new, untapped, computer-based special effect. Douglas Smythe of George Lucas's special effects division at ILM developed software for generating image-merging effects for the Ron Howard film *Willow*. This fantasy-adventure story is full of magic, including a scene in which a character changes from a human to a bird, then to a turtle, a tiger, and back again. Using the new technology, the transformation took on unprecedented realism. The age of the computer-generated morph had begun.

The wizards at ILM and another top morph house, Pacific Data Images (PDI), were pioneers in creating the software for these spectacular effects. They had to develop their own software since they were essentially inventing new technology. While morphing technology has finally become accessible to everyday users, most professional morphing effects are still done with such premium, commercial software—a full setup may cost as much as $250,000.

Since its dramatic introduction in *Willow,* morphing has become the most sought after special effect ever. It has shown up in all kinds of movies, television commercials, television programs, and music videos. Though perfectly suited for fantasy, science fiction, and horror genres, morphing has proven to be appropriate for many other categories of visual imagery, especially humor. In the 1985 comedy *Pee Wee's Big Adventure,* a truck driver named Large Marge surprised and amused most viewers when she suddenly morphed into a hideous, bug-eyed mutant for a brief moment. Any situation that describes change or any physical effect is a candidate for a good morph.

Perhaps a review of some of the more memorable morphs in recent years will inspire you to get creative with the tools provided in this book.

Morphs in Movies

Willow was the first film to feature computerized morphing, but it was soon followed by the classic adventure film *Indiana Jones and the Last Crusade,* another ILM assignment. Morphing was used to accentuate the film's excitement and enhance the sense of imminent peril. In one memorable instance, a bad guy dramatically decomposes before your stunned eyes, after unwisely choosing the wrong grail. While morphing effects have shown up in many movie genres, science-fiction and horror movies have really flexed the special effect's muscles. Classic morphs appeared in movies such as *Star Trek VI: The Undiscovered Country, The Abyss,* and perhaps most spectacularly in *Terminator 2: Judgment Day.*

Although shape shifters (creatures able to change form at will) have been featured in science-fiction stories for decades, the concept made a grand debut on the big screen in 1992's *Star Trek VI: The Undiscovered Country.* Moviegoers were awed as a beautifully exotic woman changed into a monstrous, seven-foot-tall creature, and then into an evil version of the very recognizable Captain James T. Kirk.

In the 1989 movie *The Abyss,* an alien creature at the bottom of the sea uses water molecules to communicate with humans. In one particularly poignant scene, it assumes the face of the heroine, Lindsay Brigman, then the hero, Bud Brigman, and smiles—imitating the humans perfectly.

As mentioned, the 1991 science-fiction thriller *Terminator 2: Judgment Day* used both 2-D and 3-D morphing techniques to deal with the many different transformations called for by the script. This is one of the best show-cases of high-end morphing animations. The movie is filled with stunningly smooth morphs, allowing the audience to actually witness some truly incredible transformations. Throughout the film a liquid-metal killer molds its hands into pry bars, blades, or other tools to suit its purposes, or—as perhaps the ultimate evil twin—it changes itself into duplicates of other characters. And these flawless transformations take place right before our astonished eyes.

Morphs in Television Programs

As morphing has become more available and the costs have dropped, television studios have added the special effect to their bag of weekly tricks. Whereas "Space: 1999" relied on misdirection to imply Maya's shape transformation, recent science-fiction television programs show their characters actually changing form.

"Star Trek—Deep Space 9" features a unique character, Constable Odo, who serves as a security officer on a remote outpost. He also just happens to be a shape shifter who uses his morphing skills to slide under doors, hide out as a vat of goo, or masquerade as a piece of furniture—all in the name of the law. When a dagger is thrown at Odo's head, he melts into a liquid form. The dagger, casting a reflection in the liquid on approach, passes through Odo like a high-diver through water, leaving only a small splash behind. A laser-scanned cast of actor Rene Auberjonois and mathematically derived forms of random liquid shapes are just two of the many steps it takes to create this object morph effect. Although such techniques may still be beyond the range of most enthusiasts' equipment or budgets, keep in mind that the pilot for the 1993 TV show "Babylon 5" contained several nice 2-D morphs, created with a commercial program designed for Commodore Amiga computers.

Morphs in Music Videos

The popular music industry has also embraced morphing technology; in fact, it was being used even before the advent of MTV. The label art for John Lennon and Yoko Ono's 1972 album "Somewhere in New York City" featured their images arranged in a half circle, merging together to become one, as shown in Figure 1-5. In 1984, Kevin Godley and Lyle Creme of the band 10cc created the first video of transforming faces for their single "Cry." Although it used

Figure 1-5 John and Yoko morph into one image on the "Somewhere in New York City" album label

dissolves rather than computer-generated morphs, this video recieved a lot of attention and encouraged those experimenting with morph software.

Pop superstar Michael Jackson featured metamorphosis in several of his videos. In the mini-movie companion to his hit song "Thriller," a demure Michael turns into a raging wolf as you watch. The video, directed by John Landis, uses the same techniques featured in his film *American Werewolf in London*. Rather than combining graphic images, the change is brought about by the use of bladder bags, makeup, and camera tricks. A much more recent video of Michael Jackson's, "Black or White," is a shape-shifting extravaganza from the magicians at PDI. The song's theme of racial harmony is reinforced by the series of head-and-shoulders shots that show people of various races morphing into each other. After that eye-opening scene, in the long version of the video, one of the smoothest morphs of dissimilar forms ever done is completed when Jackson morphs into a sleek black panther. PDI used their in-house morphing program to generate those sophisticated transitions between moving characters.

PDI further established their place as digital effects specialists with the production of another video for head Talking Head, David Byrne, titled "She's Mad." This showcase of morphing includes 27 different effects that make Byrne twist and shout about the pains of love. Other artists, such as Peter Gabriel, have also featured the magic of morphing in their videos.

Morphs in Commercials and Advertisements

A common showplace for morphing is television commercials. Advertisers need to make their commercials attention-getting and memorable, and morphing certainly stands out. Exxon reinvigorated its "Put a tiger in your tank" slogan by morphing a zooming Exxon-powered car into a sprinting tiger, as shown in Figure 1-6. Not to be outdone in the morph-fueled gasoline market, UNOCAL showed how cars and their owners can look alike, by transforming unique faces into unique cars. Schick needed to demonstrate that standard razor blades were all wrong for a man's face—unless it was perfectly square. They went well beyond the cubism of Picasso and Braque to create men with entirely square faces, seen in Figure 1-7, morphing into the more attractive reality of a natural shape.

To emphasize the qualities of its easy-listening format in a TV commercial, a radio station used a warp effect, which exaggerates or modifies specific aspects of a subject. In this particular ad, the distressed face of a woman reacts to various stations as she turns the radio dial. The heavy metal station makes her ears literally throb, talk radio inflates her mouth, and her eyes bulge from her head as the search becomes intolerable. Another commercial shows a bored airline passenger who seems completely lost without his video game, but a conscientious stewardess finally offers "Coffee, tea, or SEGA?!" as her eyes bug out on that final key word.

Figure 1-6 A real tiger tank?

Figure 1-7 Morphing creates a face well-suited to the conventional razor

OTHER APPLICATIONS AND POSSIBILITIES

Although the most widely recognized use of morphing is as a special effects technique in movies, television, and advertising, it is not strictly limited to these entertainment applications. As it becomes widely available, morphing could also prove an effective tool in medicine, law enforcement, and business.

◆ Image warping could be used to preview the results of corrective and cosmetic surgery. Start with a presurgery photograph of a patient and warp the nose or chin to their expected postsurgery shapes. This would definitely help patients who don't know what to expect and might help calm the apprehensive patient. Conservative surgeons might even find morphing a helpful tool in discouraging a patient from undertaking an optional procedure.

◆ Forensic scientists already use equations and statistics on tissue depth to reconstruct facial features from human skulls. These could also be used along with morphing techniques to warp images of "average" faces to match the features of murder victims. For more information on this method, see a paper called "Computer aided forensic facial reconstruction," by Ray Evenhouse, Mary Rasmussen, and Lewis Sadler of the University of Illinois at Chicago's Department of Biomedical Visualization.

◈ Morphing can be effective in artificially "aging" photographs. The technique makes it possible for police or other agencies to have a better idea of how a missing person or suspect might look years after a photo was taken. For example, you can use image warping to reshape a hairline, add wrinkles, or show the effects of physical maturity.

◈ Create special effects for business presentations, multimedia applications, and computer role-playing games. Imagine, for example, role-playing games in which a spell actually metamorphized a digitized image of the player.

◈ Develop pictures of nonexistent people and animals. Just create a single image that's halfway between "before" and "after" photos of people and animals that no longer exist.

Animation

Morphing and animation are closely linked concepts. On some rare occasions you'll be able to use a single morphed picture all by itself, but you'll almost always need to animate your results. In computer animation, you need to display many pictures, one after the other, real fast. If the pictures go by quickly enough, your eye will be fooled into seeing an actual movement instead of discrete pictures. So it goes with morphing: you've got to display the pictures quickly in sequence or your eye won't be fooled into seeing a real transformation.

Each separate picture in an animation is a frame. The speed at which the frames are displayed is called the frame rate. Frame rate is measured in frames-per-second, or fps. The frame rate for motion pictures is 24 fps. American television uses a rate of 30 fps.

A *flic* is an animation in the .FLI (or .FLC) file format. This type of file first appeared in Autodesk's Animator program, but it's now supported by many other animation programs. Some other popular animation file formats are AVI (Microsoft Video for Windows), MPEG, and ANI (Presidio's 3D Workshop).

GET READY TO EXPLORE

The ability to change shape has always been a source of intrigue. Magicians, scientists, and surgeons have all tried to transform shapes, but only with

recent morphing technology has the ability been so widely accessible. Already a mainstay of the entertainment industry, morphing technology has finally found its way to home computer systems.

Now that you are more familiar with (and perhaps inspired by) the theory and background of computer-generated morphing, get ready to learn hands-on how to create your own dazzling morphs.

2

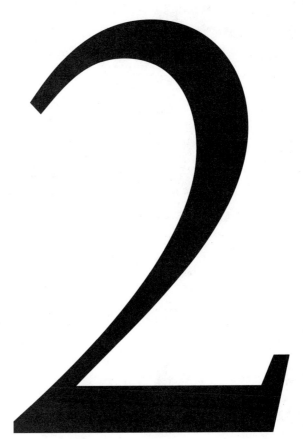

DMorf
Tutorial

CHAPTER 2

DMorf Tutorial

S o far you've learned some of the background and theory behind morphing, but you haven't actually gotten any dirt under your fingernails. In this chapter you're going to get a chance to roll up your sleeves and get some hands-on experience morphing pictures. When you're done with this tutorial, you'll have a finished morph animation sequence that you built from scratch.

The morphing development process (and this tutorial) can be broken down into six steps:

◆ Select two image files to morph, a "before" image and an "after" image.

◆ Load the pictures that you've selected into DMorf, the morphing program included with this book.

◆ Create the control mesh. A morphing program requires that you tell it the shapes of the object in your pictures, so it knows what to morph. In DMorf, you'll use a control mesh for this purpose.

◆ Build and view a short animation based on your pictures and control mesh, to test how well the mesh matches the pictures.

◆ Since a morph doesn't usually work perfectly the first time around, you'll need to fix any problems that you discovered in the test morph.

◆ When you've fixed all the problems in your control mesh, build a longer, final version of your morphing animation.

Now, let's morph!

Make sure that the directory into which the morphing tools have been copied is specified in your path. See the installation section at the beginning of this book for more information.

STEP 1: PICK TWO PICTURES

Before you can morph, you'll need to have two pictures to morph with, a "before" image and an "after" image. Picking the right pictures can sometimes take longer than morphing them. You can morph pretty much any two pictures, as long as they have the same dimensions, but it's much simpler to work with two objects that have similar features. You're going to have to create a control mesh that matches the features between the pictures, and the more dissimilar they are, the harder it will be to create the mesh. The result also looks a lot better when the before and after images aren't too different. Human heads are probably the easiest objects to morph, because most of them have two eyes, a single nose, in roughly the same place, a mouth below it, and a chin below that.

Where do you find pictures of two human heads that you can use for morphing? If you don't have a scanner or camcorder and video digitizer, then you can still download picture files from a computer bulletin board service or buy clip art on diskette or CD-ROM. If you do have such hardware, you can grab pictures from the best possible source: your family photo album. There will be more details on scanning, digitizing, and downloading in Chapter 3. For the

Figure 2-1 Before and after

purposes of this chapter, let's assume we've already chosen the pictures. Figure 2-1 shows the two pictures that we'll start with, scanned photographs of two of my favorite human heads, my nephew, Danny Dolmat, and brother-in-law, George Dolmat.

STEP 2: START UP DMORF

The instructions in this tutorial are aimed at people using vanilla MS-DOS. If you want to run from Microsoft Windows or IBM's OS/2, so that you can access more memory, you'll first have to open up a full-screen DOS window. In Windows, click on the MS-DOS icon. In OS/2, click on the Full-Screen DOS window. A DOS prompt will appear on your screen, and from this point on things will operate exactly the same as if you were running in DOS.

Once you've selected your pictures, you are ready to start the morphing program. Switch to the directory that contains the picture files. In this tutorial, you'll be

Figure 2-2 The DMorf screen

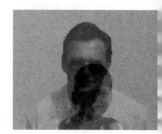

Figure 2-3 Fading

morphing some pictures from the disks included with this book, DANNY.TGA and GEORGE.TGA, so switch to the CHAP2 directory by typing

```
cd\morphing\chap2
```

When you're in the appropriate directory, you can start DMorf and start merging the images. Type the DMorf command, along with the filenames of the pictures. For this tutorial, type

```
dmorf danny.tga george.tga
```

DMorf starts up, and it reads and displays the two pictures in side-by-side windows. (Note that DMorf can read a few image file formats other than the TGA format used in this example; it can also handle GIF and IMG files.) It displays the pictures in shades of gray, regardless of the original color format, but DMorf performs all of its other processing in full color. It resizes the pictures so that they fit in the windows, but creates output pictures in the original size.

DMorf picks default values for such settings as the number of in-between pictures to create, output file format, and so on. As you'll learn later, you can change these settings at any time, but let's stick with the defaults for this exercise. Figure 2-2 displays DMorf's startup screen.

STEP 3: CREATE THE CONTROL MESH

Make sure your mouse driver is loaded before running DMorf.

If you were to go ahead and click on the Go button right now, DMorf would attempt to morph between these two pictures. You would end up with the rather miserable-looking results shown in Figure 2-3, a simple fade between the two pictures. Fading is only one half of morphing. The other half, warping, requires a control mesh.

A *control mesh* is a kind of grid of lines connecting corresponding points in the two pictures. The locations of these intersection points can be moved around to make the lines follow the contours of the objects in your pictures, defining the geometry of the scenes so that DMorf knows what to move where.

You can add lines to the control mesh by moving the mouse cursor into the border around one of the picture windows and clicking the right mouse button. The result is a line that goes across to the point clicked, either vertically from the top border to the bottom, or horizontally from the left border to the right. To add a vertical line, place the cursor in the border above or below the window. Figure 2-4 shows the DMorf picture windows after a single vertical line has been added.

Figure 2-4 Adding a vertical line

Add two more vertical lines, one on the other side of the face, and another right down the middle. To add a horizontal line, place the cursor in the border to the left or right of one of the pictures and click the right mouse button. Figure 2-5 shows a horizontal line being added to the mesh.

So what have we got now? Just a bunch of straight lines overlaying the pictures. To control the morphing process, the lines have to follow the contours of the objects in the scene. To do this, you need to move the intersection points of the horizontal and vertical lines of the mesh so that they identify key points in the picture.

Just move the mouse cursor so it's pointing at one of the intersections, and click on the left mouse button. While holding down the mouse button, move the mouse. The intersection point will move to wherever you move the mouse cursor. When you're satisfied with the position of the intersection, release the button. Figure 2-6 shows the pictures and their control mesh after a few points have been moved to map Danny's chin.

The locations of the intersections don't stay the same across the two pictures. You need to move the control points so that they cover corresponding features in the two pictures. If the intersection of the bottommost horizontal line from the bottom and the middle vertical line in the left picture points to

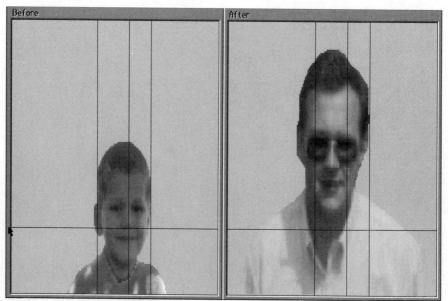

Figure 2-5 Adding a horizontal line

Figure 2-6 Moving the vertices around

Danny's chin, then the intersection of the second horizontal line from the bottom and the middle vertical line in the right picture must point to George's chin. Figure 2-7 shows the mesh after all of the points that we've added so far have been placed with their intersections in corresponding locations.

So far we've only mapped the general shape of the heads. To create a convincing morph, we're going to have to do more than that. Add some more lines to the mesh so that there are more intersections to work with, and make those lines follow some more of the contours in the faces. Figure 2-8 shows the meshes after the shoulders, hairline, nose, collar, and mouth have been mapped.

Because it's difficult to follow curves precisely using straight lines, DMorf actually uses curved lines called *splines* to connect the intersections, rather than the straight line segments that you see now. Because curved lines take longer to display on the screen, DMorf doesn't use the curved lines while you're editing points. It waits until it's time to perform the morph. You can find out ahead of time what the curved lines look like by clicking on the Splines button in the menu at the bottom of the screen. Figure 2-9 shows the Spline view for the current mesh.

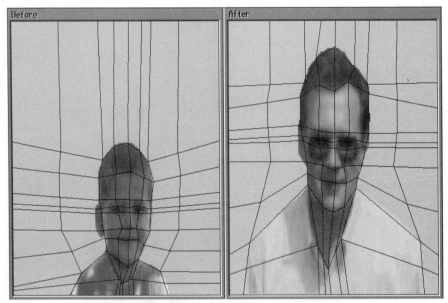

Figure 2-7   Matching features

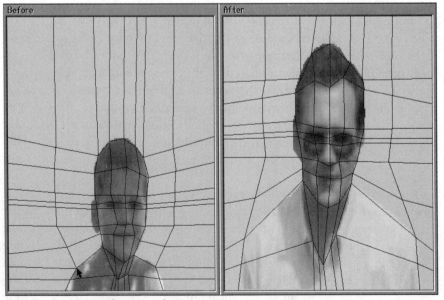

Figure 2-8   A tighter mesh

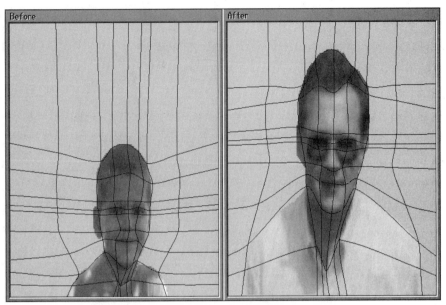

Figure 2-9 Spline view

A spline is a curve defined by just a few points. Using those control points and a mathematical equation, a program can compute new points that lie along the curve. There are a bunch of different kinds of splines, in both two and three dimensions. Some use *approximation:* the curve passes near each of the points, but usually doesn't pass through them. Others use *interpolation:* the curve passes through each and every point that defines it. DMorf uses a variety of 2-D interpolative spline called a Catmull-Rom spline.

When we display the splines defined by these control points, we see a few problems. Some of the curves, especially those near the shoulders and the top of George's head, just don't follow the contours that they're supposed to. We'll need to modify the curves to fix this. The way to do this is to add some more lines to the mesh to give more intersection points to fiddle with, and move them around until the Spline view's curves more closely match the edges of the objects in the scene. Another problem is that there aren't any lines at all covering the ears. To fix that, just add another line and move the intersections into position. Figure 2-10 shows a more tightly controlled mesh for the two pictures. Figure 2-11 shows the Spline view for the modified mesh. Looks better, doesn't it?

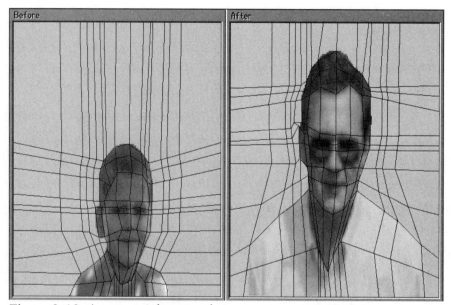

Figure 2-10 An even tighter mesh

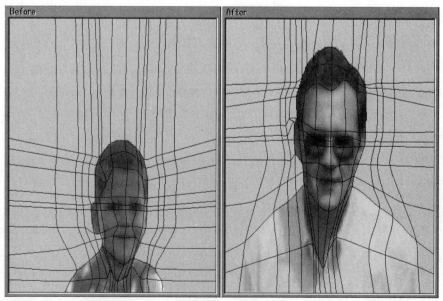

Figure 2-11 Spline view of the tighter mesh

Figure 2-12 Saving the mesh to a file

Now we have a workable control mesh, and we're almost ready to morph. This is a very good time to save your work. Strange things can happen: cats have been known to reboot unattended computers; power can fail; and, though it's rare, DMorf can crash and dump you out to the DOS prompt. So click on the Save button in the menu. DMorf will present you with a dialog box, as shown in Figure 2-12.

Type a filename for the mesh, DG.MSH, and press (ENTER). The first part of the filename can be anything up to eight letters, but it should be something that's easy to remember. In this case, "D" is for Danny and "G" is for George. The extension should always be .MSH. DMorf saves both meshes and all of your settings.

STEP 4: TEST THE MORPH

Just click on the Go button in the menu, and DMorf will get to work. For each output frame (the number of frames is based on the value in the Frames number box in the menu), DMorf will create an in-between mesh from the two user-created meshes, and deform both pictures so that the shapes in them line up in their new positions. Then it averages the colors in the two pictures to come up with a new picture to save to disk. The screen should look like Figure 2-13 during the morphing process.

If you have a fast computer with a math coprocessor, this will be done in a minute or two. Otherwise it could take considerably longer. When it's all done, you'll have five new picture files, in Targa format, of the frames between DANNY.TGA and GEORGE.TGA. They will be named MORF0001.TGA, MORF0002.TGA, and so on, up to MORF0005.TGA. Leave DMorf by clicking the mouse on the Quit button.

Build a Flic

You've got a bunch of still images sitting on your hard disk doing nothing interesting. To get them moving, you've got to turn them into a flic animation

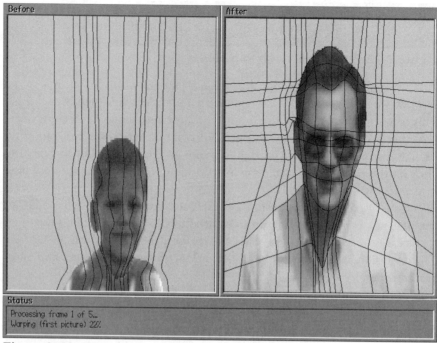

Figure 2-13 Morphing at last!

file. Use DTA (Dave's TGA Animator), the second program included with this book, to compile those TGA files into a flic animation file. DTA is covered in detail in Chapter 4, but you don't need to know all of its options just to build a flic. For now, just type this command while in the MORPHING\CHAP2 directory:

```
dta morf*.tga /omorph1
```

Figure 2-14 Results of the morph

The first parameter tells DTA to read all of the files in the current directory that begin with the letters "MORF". There's no /F (file format) switch on this command line, so DTA will create output in the default flic format. The /O switch tells DTA to use "morph1" in the output filename, so DTA will generate a file called MORPH1.FLI.

Display the Flic

You've built a flic from your morph sequence, but you need to use a viewer program to see the result. The Trilobyte program, Play, is included with this book. Play is described more fully in Chapter 4, but you can use it now to display the results of your morph. Display the flic you just created with Play, by typing the command:

```
play morph1.fli
```

Slow the flic display down by pressing ⑤ on your keyboard. The sequence should look like the pictures in Figure 2-14. When you've looked at the flic long enough, press (ESC) to exit play.

STEP 5: REFINE THE MESH

After seeing the morph, you've probably noticed some weird artifacts in the sequence. Things don't quite line up in several places, especially the hair on top of the head. So let's go back into DMorf and clean them up. You could start up DMorf just like before with the picture filenames, and then use the Load button to load the meshes you saved earlier, but you can save yourself a few seconds by just typing the name of the mesh file on the command line instead of the names of the pictures:

```
dmorf dg.msh
```

DMorf will start up again, and you'll be right back where you were at the end of step 3, with the two pictures in their side-by-side windows, overlaid by the two meshes. It's kind of hard to see how the mesh could be improved, because the points appear to match the shapes very well. We need to take a closer look at the pictures and the mesh of control points. Use the mouse to press the Max button at the bottom of the screen, and DMorf will display a much larger view of the picture from the left window, as in Figure 2-15.

Because the picture is larger than in the regular view, but the thickness of the mesh lines stays the same, you can more easily see any gaps between the lines and the curves that they're supposed to match. You also have finer control over the point locations. Now you can see that the line segments around the ear don't match that shape very well, so the control points need a bit of adjustment. The points on the sides of the head could use some tweaking too.

Switch to a maximized view of the other picture by clicking on the Other button. You'll see the picture displayed in Figure 2-16.

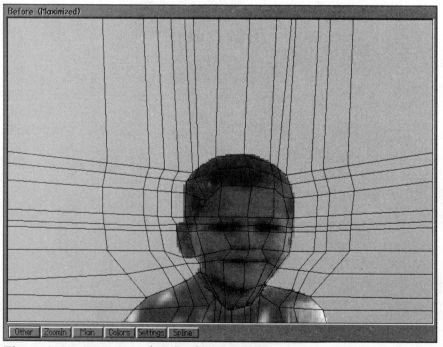

Figure 2-15 Max view for the first picture

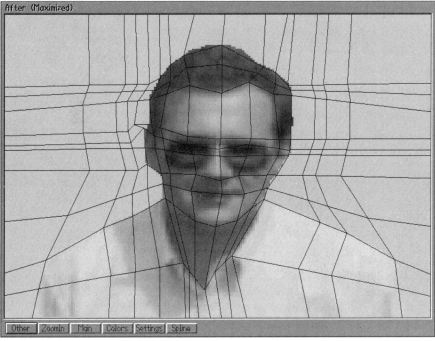

Figure 2-16 Maximized view for the second picture

The main problems here are at the top of the head, where the line breaks into segments. There aren't quite enough control points to get the curve just right, so you need to add a few extra control points by inserting new vertical lines. But the lines on the top of the head weren't all *that* far off. So why, when we ran that test morph, was there an extra blur of hair stretched several pixels over the top of the head? Probably because George's head is so much closer to the top of the picture than Danny's is. The small gap between the top of George's head and the top of the screen gets stretched to fill much more space, and the pixels that represent the top of his head get stretched too. You can prevent this from happening by adding another horizontal line to the mesh very close above his head. The background pixels above that new line will get stretched instead. Figure 2-17 shows a Spline view of the mesh modified in this manner.

Save a new mesh file, as DG2.MSH, and click on the Go button. After it's done morphing, exit DMorf and run DTA against the TGA files again, and play the flic. As Figure 2-18 shows, it's a lot smoother.

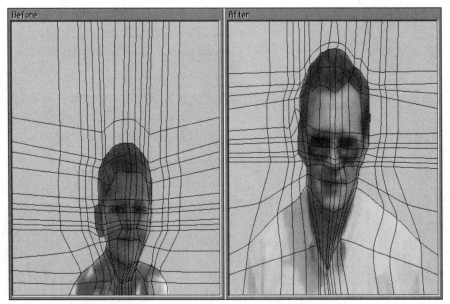

Figure 2-17 Spline view

If you're satisfied with how the morph looks now, then go ahead to step 6. If not, adjust the mesh some more.

STEP 6: THE FINAL MORPH

So far for testing purposes, we've only been creating five frames of the morph sequence. That's enough to judge how well the morph looks, but it's not

Figure 2-18 The final morph

enough to generate a smooth animation. Instead, there are very noticeable jumps between the frames. It looks a lot like a bad strobe effect. Broadcast television blasts out 30 frames every second, for very smooth movement. A 10-second morph would require 300 frames, which takes up a lot of disk space and takes a long time to generate. Most computers can't keep up with a frame rate that high. So we don't have to get quite *that* carried away. Fifty frames should do the job rather nicely, and 20 will do in a pinch.

Let's continue with the tutorial, and try to smooth out the morph we've been developing. Reload the pictures and meshes into DMorf:

```
dmorf dg.msh
```

Now click on the button labeled Settings in the File menu. DMorf will display the Settings dialog, which includes a number box labeled Frames. Click the mouse button while the cursor is pointing inside of the Frames number box. DMorf will place a cursor inside of the box, allowing you to type in a different number. If you've got a fast computer and coprocessor, type the number 50 and press (ENTER). Otherwise try a smaller number, like 15 or 20, so that it will be finished during this century. Click on the Done button to close the Settings dialog. Back at the main screen, click on the Go button and wait for DMorf to morph all of the frames. (Or go for coffee or mow the lawn.) Afterward, exit DMorf and type this longer DTA command line:

```
dta danny.tga morf*.tga george.tga /p /moorph2 /s5
```

You need to supply the names of the before and after pictures in addition to the new files, because DMorf only creates output pictures of the in-between frames. The /P switch tells DTA to create a Ping-Pong flic, in which the pictures get placed in the flic twice, the second time in reverse order. The /O parameter causes the resulting flic to be named MORPH2.FLI. The /S5 tells DTA to put a speed setting of 5 into the flic's header area. Later on this will

tell Play how fast to display the flic. The unit 5 means it will display each frame for 5/70 of a second.

Play the new MORPH2.FLI and compare the result with the earlier MORPH1.FLI. Because of the additional frames you generated, it should look much smoother. When you're done viewing, press (ESC) to leave Play.

If the flic played too quickly or too slowly, the speed setting specified with DTA's /S switch wasn't right. You could change the speed in Play by pressing number keys as you did in step 4, but that won't be a permanent fix. The next time you play the flic, you'll have to readjust the speed.

To permanently change the speed setting, you could retype the DTA command and supply a different number with the /S parameter. The problem with that solution is that it takes so long. Why rebuild the whole flic just to change one little number at the beginning of the file? Fortunately you don't have to. Along with DTA, you'll find a utility program called FLISPEED.EXE in your C:\MORPHING\TOOLS directory. FLISPEED can change the speed setting in a FLI or FLC file without rebuilding it from scratch. It runs very quickly because all it does is modify a single number. Type the FLISPEED command, along with the name of the flic file and a new speed switch:

```
flispeed morph2.fli /s4
```

FLISPEED will patch the flic file with the new speed setting almost instantly. Play MORPH2.FLI again to see if the new play rate is perfect. If not, repeat the FLISPEED/PLAY cycle until it is.

SUMMARY

In this chapter, you learned how to use the morphing tools in their basic form. Now you know what a mesh is and how to build one. You've learned how to create a simple morph, build a flic from it, and play it back. Perhaps most impressive, you transformed a 6-year-old boy into a 30-year-old man; then changed him back again! Not a bad day's work. Ponce de Leon searched for the fountain of youth for years and never came this close.

You're off to a great start. Now that you've experienced simple morphing, it's time to learn some advanced techniques. Applying some neat, but relatively simple, tricks to a basic morph turns it into a sophisticated special effect, and provides you with a great means to get truly creative on your computer.

3

Tricks and Techniques

CHAPTER 3

Tricks and Techniques

The essential elements of morphing can be learned quickly. You've already completed the basics steps of changing one graphic image into another by defining, building, and playing a simple morphing animation. It is the enhancements that give those truly eye-opening morphs their breathtaking punch. Just like frosting can turn a cake into a masterpiece, advanced tweaks can turn a simple morph into an awesome transformation.

You can use the same tricks the pros use to make truly sophisticated special effects. In this chapter you'll learn a number of ways to fine-tune the development process, explore special effects, and add polish and pizzazz to your morphs. Now that you can create a basic morph, you're ready to go from hamburger to steak (or turn a hamburger *into* steak). You'll learn now to:

- ◆ Capture your own images
- ◆ Speed up the process of developing morphs
- ◆ Deal with differences in lighting between the before and after images
- ◆ Eradicate distracting background features that can wreck some morphs
- ◆ Create caricatures, moving objects, and other special image-warping effects

◆❯ String several morphs into a single sequence

◆❯ Output the results of your work to video

SOURCES

There are a number of image files on the disks that accompany this book, which are provided to complement the examples in the text. But they're probably not going to be enough. When it's time to create your own morphs, you're going to need pictures that fit your own artistic vision. You'll want to morph images of your own family members, friends, pets, and co-workers. You'll want background images that set just the right mood. How do you find or create more pictures to work with? Read on.

Scan Them

A scanner is probably the single most useful piece of hardware that you can add to your system to help you get pictures into your computer. With a scanner, you can convert your photographs and drawings into image files. With a flatbed scanner, you can place a sheet of paper or an open book face-down against a glass plate, and read the images from the paper right into software that comes supplied with the scanner. Figure 3-1 shows one flatbed scanner, a Hewlett-Packard Scanjet IIc. Color flatbed scanners start at about $900. This particular scanner can be purchased from mail-order vendors (advertised in computer magazines like *PC Magazine* or *Computer Shopper*) for about $1300.

With a hand scanner, you move the scanner itself, which looks something like a large mouse, across the page. They're a lot cheaper than flatbed scanners (they can cost anywhere from about $100 for the cheapest 32-shade grayscale scanner, up to around $550 for a good true-color model). They're limited, however, to capturing smaller pictures, and they require a steady hand for good results. Figure 3-2 shows a hand scanner.

Video Digitizers

Another great source for morphing material is video. With a video digitizer board, you can connect your computer to your VCR or camcorder, and pull

Figure 3-1 Scanning with a flatbed scanner

Figure 3-2 A hand scanner in action

any image that can be displayed on your television screen right into your PC. The image quality won't be as good as it is with a scanner, because television signals are low resolution; but it takes a lot less time to record something with a camcorder and capture the image than it does to photograph it, get the film developed, and scan the photo.

One such board, Gatz und Hartmann's PC-Hurricane Moviegrabber, fits into a half-length expansion slot and connects to your video equipment with a standard RCA cable. Start up the capture program that comes with the board (the PC-Hurricane comes with two: one for DOS and one for Windows), and it displays the video in almost real time in a window. Tell it to record, and the software captures a series of television frames into memory as 16-bit images. The number of frames it can store at one time is limited by the size of the window (up to about 320 x 240 for American NTSC television, or 384 x 288 for European PAL) and by the amount of memory you've got in your machine. You can store individual frames as BMP files (in the Windows version) or TGA files (in the DOS version), or store the whole sequence. The PC-Hurricane can be ordered directly from Gatz und Hartmann for $499. Contact them at:

> Gatz und Hartmann
> Ingenieurbuero fuer Multimedia-Anwendungen
> Fehrbelliner Str. 32
> W-1000 Berlin 20
> Germany
> Telephone & fax: ++ 49 30 375 55 68
> email to: harti@mikro.ee.tu-berlin.de

Other products are available at similar prices, such as Creative Labs' VideoSpigot for Windows (phone number 1-408-428-6600). The suggested retail price for a similar product from MediaVision, ProMovie Studio, is about $450. You can contact them at:

> MediaVision
> 3185 Laurel View Court
> Fremont, CA   94538
> For direct sales, telephone: (800) 684-6699

A trick that was very useful in the development of this book was to record an object from a variety of different positions, then to capture 200 frames or so at a time, and weed out the one or two best-looking frames to save as an image file. Waste as much videotape as you feel like, because you can always record over it later.

Rendering

If you don't want to morph objects that exist in the real world, you can always create synthetic images using a rendering program. This type of software allows you to take photorealistic snapshots of scenes that exist only as three-dimensional models inside your computer. Some of the more popular commercial ren-

Figure 3-3 Image rendered with Polyray

dering programs on the market are 3D-Studio (Autodesk), 3D Workshop (Presidio), and Will Vinton's Playmation (Hash Enterprises). Some freeware and shareware alternatives are the POV-Ray ray tracer, which is described in *Image Lab*, by Tim Wegner and *Ray Tracing Creations*, by Drew Wells and Chris Young (both published by Waite Group Press). Alexander Enzmann's Polyray is explored in *Making Movies on Your PC* by David Mason and Alexander Enzmann and *Animation How-To CD*, by Jeff Bowermaster (also published by Waite Group Press). Stephen Coy's Vivid raytracer is available as shareware. All are also available in CompuServe's GRAPHDEV forum and on The Graphics Alternative BBS. (See the following section, Bulletin Boatds and Online Services.) Figure 3-3 shows one such rendered image.

Copyright Concerns

If you're just morphing for the fun of it, and don't plan to do anything with your results beyond enjoying them yourself and showing them to friends and family, then it should be safe to do whatever you want with any pictures you scan or download. But if you intend to use them for commercial purposes, or upload your flics to a bulletin board, you should be careful not to infringe people's copyrights. Pictures in magazines, frames from television shows and movies, and artwork all *belong* to somebody, and those somebodies have legal rights to their material. If you have pictures that you didn't scan from your own photographs, didn't model and render yourself, or didn't draw yourself; if they aren't labeled public domain, or you haven't gotten permission to use them, then don't use those pictures except for your own enjoyment.

Bulletin Boards and Online Services

If you have a modem and communications software, you can access a huge library of picture files with a telephone call. There are thousands of bulletin board services (BBSs) that you can dial up, all over the world. Unless you live on a desert island deep in the Pacific, there are sure to be plenty of them right in your area code. Some allow free access, and others charge an annual fee. Many bulletin boards have file sections containing thousands of pictures in the ultra-popular GIF file format, ready to be downloaded. You can usually find out the telephone numbers of local BBSs by asking around at computer stores and computer clubs. Once you've accessed one BBS, you can almost always get numbers for others by downloading a BBS list.

If you're looking for scanned photographs, try the local boards. If you're interested in computer-generated art, then two great BBS systems that you might like to try out are The Graphics Alternative in El Cerrito, California, at (510) 521-2780, and You Can Call Me Ray in Palatine, Illinois, at (708) 358-5611. Both have large libraries of rendered art.

CompuServe, a nationwide online service, has a massive collection of GIF files in its Graphics Forums (use the GO GRAPHICS command to access these). CompuServe charges are based on the amount of time you're connected, so it is much more expensive to use than a local bulletin board. However, the size and quality of their collection is probably unmatched. Often you'll find a booklet with CompuServe membership information included with the documentation for your modem or communications software. If not, you can purchase a membership kit from most computer stores.

Some other online services that allow file downloading include America OnLine, BIX (Byte Information Exchange), and GEnie. Prodigy, unfortunately, doesn't support downloading.

CD-ROMs

A number of entrepreneurs publish image libraries on CD-ROMs. If you have a CD-ROM player you can buy a disk containing hundreds of megabytes of picture files. They're available at most software stores, and also from mail-order suppliers. These pictures come from a variety of sources: some come from magazine publishers' archives, others are simply collections of pictures that are available from many bulletin board systems. Make sure to read the fine print on the packaging: CD-ROM collections usually come with restrictions on how you can legally use the images.

FASTER PROCESSING

You'll discover as you experiment with DMorf that morphing can be a pretty slow process. Even if you have a fast computer, it can take hours to produce a complete morphing sequence. However, if you're willing to put up with reduced picture quality, there are a number of ways to speed things up. In general, do all your test runs using the fastest possible settings and options. When you're finally satisfied with how it's working, *then* rerun the morph with the slower high-quality settings while you get some sleep. Here are some specific tricks you can use for faster morphing:

◆ *Create fewer frames.* Even if you intend to produce a 100-frame morph animation, that doesn't mean you have to generate all 100 frames every time you try a test run. Set the number in the Frames box to a low number, like 4 or 5. Only set it at 100 when you're ready for the final morph.

◆ *Start small.* The larger your pictures are, the longer it will take DMorf to morph them. A set of 640 x 480 images takes almost five times longer to morph than a set of 320 x 200 images, and more than 19 times longer than 160 x 100 images. So while you're developing your mesh, use down-scaled versions of your larger pictures. Use DTA (Dave's Targa Animator, described in Chapter 4) to resize each picture:

```
dta picture1.tga /sc160,100 /ft /osmall1
dta picture2.tga /sc160,100 /ft /osmall2
```

◆ The /SC command-line option tells DTA to rescale the pictures down to 160 x 100 pixels. The /FT option tells DTA to create its output in Targa format instead of the default Flic format. The /O options tell it what to call the new files. DTA will create new, smaller versions of your pictures called SMALL1.TGA and SMALL2.TGA. Create a mesh using these smaller pictures, test-morph with the smaller pictures, and switch back to the full-size pictures when you're ready to run the final morph.

◆ *Use the quickest settings.* Several options on the Morphing Switches menu panel have default settings that cause DMorf to produce nicer output, but they can slow things down considerably. The Smooth Resampling option is a particular time drain, so switch it off for all of your test runs. The morphed frames will have a chunky look to them, but you'll get them faster.

LIGHTING

When you morph between two objects, it's very important to pay attention to the lighting in the scenes. With morphing, you're attempting to create an illusion, and you don't want anything to spoil the effect. It's much like a stage magician's trick—the effect is destroyed if someone forgets to close the trap door, or if the magician's sleeve starts leaking playing cards. It can be just as disconcerting to see a shadow disappear from the left side of a morphing head and suddenly reappear on the right, or to morph from a brightly lit object to a dimly lit picture containing heavy shadows. The easiest solution to such problems is to start with pictures that are similarly lit. If that isn't an option, sometimes you can fix such problems by fiddling with your pictures.

If one of your pictures is too much darker or lighter than the other, you can modify the picture's brightness. Use DTA's /GA (gamma-correction) function, which is discussed in Chapter 4, to lighten or darken the image. If you own a general purpose paint or image-processing program, such as Adobe's Photoshop or ZSoft's PhotoFinish, then you have more sophisticated tools available to you. Photoshop, for example, has a menu of six different methods for adjusting color, brightness, and contrast.

Figure 3-4 Sphere-to-cube morph, with ruined background

If shadow orientation doesn't match across two pictures, you can sometimes just flip one of the pictures horizontally. In DMorf, you can use the Edit button to switch to an editing screen, click on the FlipH button to flip it, and click on the Save button to update the picture file. Or click on SaveAs if you want to save the picture under a new filename. Image-processing programs like those mentioned in the previous paragraph usually have a host of flipping and rotating features. Of course, this trick will only work for pictures that are somewhat symmetrical.

One last trick you can try (if you have Photoshop) is to remove the shadows completely. Photoshop's "dodge" and "burn" features allow you to use the mouse like a paintbrush that brightens or darkens small areas of your picture.

THE BACKGROUND PROBLEM

One troublesome problem is that the morphing program doesn't understand the difference between foreground and background. If there is anything at all in the background it gets warped and blended along with the objects that you care about. Even if two pictures have identical backgrounds, they will be wrecked when the images are warped, to make the foreground objects line up. Figure 3-4 illustrates the problem. The foreground shapes morph fine, but the twisting checkerboard ruins the effect.

The simplest solution is to edit out the backgrounds with an image editor. You can use a high-end editing tool like Photoshop or PhotoFinish, if you've got one; but any paint program, including the Paintbrush program that comes with Microsoft Windows, can do the job almost as well. Just paint the background over with a single color, save, and morph. Figure 3-5 shows the improved results. It's better, but it sure looks boring with no background at all!

  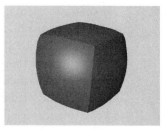

Figure 3-5 Sphere-to-cube morph, with no background

Another solution is more difficult, but the improved results are often worth the extra effort: make the background transparent, and overlay the morphed frames on a new background. The usual method of representing pixel colors, RGB color, or 24-bit color, uses three separate numbers to store the red, green, and blue components, and allows your computer to specify any color that you can imagine. DMorf uses another method, called RGB α (pronounced "R-G-B-alpha"), which uses four byte-sized numbers. The first three work the same as in RGB color, but the last one, the *alpha* byte, represents transparency. This extra byte in each pixel is usually called the *alpha channel*, or a *mask*. The process of overlaying a picture that has an alpha channel of another picture is called *compositing*. When you use DTA to composite images, it performs calculations on that alpha byte to decide how much of the foreground image and how much of the background image to blend together to make each new pixel. If a pixel's alpha value is set at 0, then it'll only use the pixel from the background image. If the pixel's alpha is set to 255, then it'll only use the foreground color. Otherwise, it will blend the two colors together.

The Targa file format (in its 32-bit variety) is the only one supported by DMorf and DTA that can contain an alpha channel. It has to be a 32-bit, or 4 bytes per pixel, Targa, because it has to hold all three regular color components plus an alpha byte. Note to 80286 users: the number of bits per pixel has *nothing* to do with the number of bits in your processor's data path.

Creating Pictures with Transparency

A few rendering programs, including Autodesk's 3D-Studio and Alexander Enzmann's shareware ray tracer, Polyray, can generate picture files containing transparency information (in an alpha channel) to mask out the background. All you have to do is tell the program to create a 32-bit Targa file, and refrain from placing anything behind the foreground objects.

Adding Transparency to Preexisting Pictures

Some high-end paint and image-processing programs, including Adobe's PhotoShop, allow you to add alpha masks to your pictures using paint tools. Not everybody can afford to purchase one of these programs, however, so DMorf contains an alpha-editing facility that lets you do the same thing. It isn't as sophisticated as PhotoShop's, but it can do the job. There are two methods for masking out backgrounds: painting and chroma-keying.

Painting a Mask

We'll start with a picture of my nephew Danny and niece Sarah, D&S.TGA. Later on in this chapter, we're going to morph Danny into Sarah and vice versa simultaneously, but the background in this picture gets in the way.

On DMorf's main screen, click the Edit button. DMorf will read the whole picture into memory (if it hasn't already done so because of the /PRELOAD command-line switch) and display it in a full-screen window with no control mesh superimposed. On this Edit screen, you can select a rectangular area of the picture to make transparent. Move the mouse cursor to one corner of the area that you want to mask and click the left mouse button. Hold the mouse button down while you move the cursor over to the opposite corner of the area that you're masking. As Figure 3-6 shows, DMorf will draw a box on the screen showing the rectangle that you're selecting.

When you release the mouse cursor, DMorf will modify that area of the picture to make it transparent, and display those pixels using the Alpha Color from the Colors dialog. Figure 3-7 shows the modified screen.

Draw more boxes to mask out the rest of the background. Don't get too close to the edges of the foreground objects, though, because a tool as heavy-handed as this one is liable to chop off pieces that shouldn't be chopped off.

Figure 3-6 Selecting an area to mask

Figure 3-7 Masked-out area

You'll get a chance to fine-tune later. Figure 3-8 displays the picture with some more of the background masked out.

When you've got all the wide-open areas filled in, it's time to switch to a tool with finer control: Zoom mode. Click on the ZoomIn button on the bottom of the screen. Move the cursor to one corner of an area that you want to fine-tune, and then press and hold down the mouse button. Move the mouse

Figure 3-8 Partially masked picture

Figure 3-9 Selecting an area to edit

cursor some more. You'll see a highlighted rectangle between the first point that you selected and wherever you move the cursor to. Figure 3-9 shows the zoom selection box.

When the rectangle covers the area that you want to zoom in on, release the mouse button. DMorf will zoom in on the area that you selected, as shown in Figure 3-10. Now you can use the mouse to mask out individual pixels.

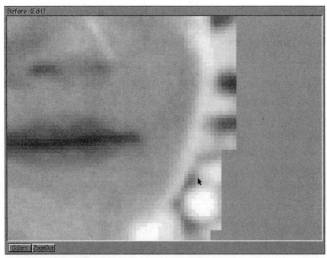

Figure 3-10 Zoomed editing screen

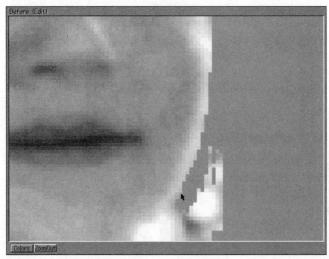

Figure 3-11 Editing in zoom mode

Move the mouse cursor to a magnified pixel that isn't part of Danny's head and click the mouse button. DMorf will make that pixel transparent and display it on the screen in the Mask Color. Figure 3-11 shows the zoomed-in picture after most of the background pixels have been made transparent.

When you're finished masking the pixels in that zoomed-in area, click on the ZoomOut button on the menu at the bottom of the screen to return to the

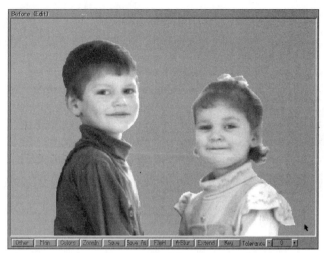

Figure 3-12 Fully-masked background

regular Edit screen. Click on ZoomIn again and select another area. Edit the pixels in the new zoomed-in area. Keep doing this until the entire background is masked. Figure 3-12 displays the picture of Danny and Sarah once the entire background has been made transparent.

Save your work. While still in the editing screen, click on the SaveAs button and type DSL.TGA at the Fileneame prompt.

Chroma-Keying

Another way to deal with the "background problem" is used in TV weather reports. Most television weather reporters these days deliver their prognostications while standing in front of a moving weather map. Sorry to dispel any illusions you might have, but there isn't really a map there. It's just a screen of some uniform color. Traditionally, this is a blue screen, but it could be any color at all. Special effects equipment processes the video image to replace all occurrences of that color with a video image of the weather map. This technique is called *chroma-keying,* or the *blue-screen method.*

Weatherpeople must be very careful about their wardrobes. If they stood in front of an orange screen, wearing an orange sweater, the sweater would disappear along with the background, and the audience would just see a head and hands floating in front of the weather map.

Chroma-keying has also been commonly used to place highway footage in the windows of cars in TV cop shows, so that the private eye or police officer looks like he's traveling to the scene of a crime or chasing a villain, when he's really just sitting inside of a stationary car in a soundstage. In adventure and science-fiction films, chroma-keying is often used to superimpose flying super-heroes over images of the sky, or model spaceships in front of a starfield.

DMorf can use this same trick to wipe out the backgrounds of some of your pictures. Such pictures must contain a foreground object in front of a back-ground that's made up of a single color or narrow range of colors. Because of this requirement, your pictures will generally be posed, photographed and scanned (or otherwise captured) specifically for the purpose of chroma-keying. Or you might use pictures that you've rendered using a tool, such as POV-Ray or Vivid, which doesn't save transparency in an alpha channel when it creates images; or that you've edited with a paint program that doesn't support the alpha channel.

Figure 3-13 shows BIKE.TGA, an image file provided on the disks that accompany this book. If you followed the instructions in "Installation," at the beginning of the book, you'll find it on your hard disk, in the C:\MORPHING\CHAP3 directory. It's a miniature model of a motorcycle, recorded with a camcorder in front of a bright yellow background, and cap-tured to an image file using a PC-Hurricane video digitizer (described earlier in this chapter). Because the background is all yellow, and there's no yellow in the motorcycle itself, it should work very well with chroma-keying.

Figure 3-13 BIKE.TGA

Let's give it a try. Switch to the MORPHING\CHAP3 directory and load BIKE.TGA into DMorf by typing:

```
dmorf bike.tga
```

On DMorf's main screen, click the Edit button. DMorf will load the whole picture into memory and display it in a full-screen editing window. On the editing screen, click on the Key button. Move the mouse cursor into the picture and position it over one of the background pixels. Press the mouse button, and DMorf will make all of the pixels in the picture which contain that pixel's exact color transparent. They'll display on your screen with the color defined in the Colors dialog's Alpha Color number boxes. Since most of the pixels in the background won't exactly match that one pixel that you selected, most of the background will be untouched. So increase the number in the Tol number box at the bottom-right corner of the editing screen to about 25 or so, and try keying another background pixel. The rest of the background should turn transparent. Save the picture back to disk by clicking either the Save button (if you want to save it under the original filename), or SaveAs (if you want to supply a new filename).

You can also do your chroma-keying with DTA, if you prefer, and if you know how to specify a number in RGB format. Any color you could see or imagine can be described with a combination of three numbers, representing the red, green, and blue components of that color, each ranging from 0 to 255. You can get yellow by mixing pure red and green, so you could specify yellow by using the numbers 255,255, and 0. At the DOS command line, type:

```
dta bike.tga /ft /b32 /obike2 /ch255,255,0 /ct25
```

The first parameter, BIKE.TGA, supplies the name of the input file. The switches perform the following functions:

◈ /FT tells DTA to create a new Targa-format file instead of building a flic.

◈ /B32 says that it should be a 32-bit Targa file instead of the normal 24-bit kind.

◈ /OBIKE2 provides a filename, BIKE2, for the Targa output file.

◈ /CH255,255,0 tells DTA what color to use for chroma-keying.

◈ /CT provides the chroma-key color tolerance.

You'll end up with a new image file called BIKE2.TGA in which the yellow pixels in the background have been made transparent.

Compositing

Once you've masked out a picture's original background, either by painting it or by chroma-keying, you can use DTA to overlay the masked image onto a new background. Type:

```
dta clouds.tga /l dsl.tga /ft /ocomped
```

The /L (layer) parameter following the filename of the background image (CLOUDS.TGA, an image of a cloudy sky) and the filename of the foreground picture (DSL.TGA, which we created a few pages back) separates those two pictures into two different layers, with the second layer going on top of the first. Everything that you masked out in DMorf's editing screen will be transparent, allowing the background to show through. The /FT parameter causes DTA to create a Targa-format file instead of a flic, and /OCOMPED tells it to use COMPED as the new filename. DTA will figure out on its own that it should add ".TGA" to the end of the filename. Figure 3-14 shows the final result.

When you morph two pictures that both have alpha channels, DMorf merges them just like it does pixel colors, to create a new alpha channel for each output frame. Then you can overlay whole morph sequences on top of new backgrounds. Make sure that the 32-bit TGA setting in the Pictures dialog is on, or the new alpha channel won't be saved in the TGA output files. If, instead of a single foreground picture, you had a series of morphed frames, you can composite the whole sequence onto a background with DTA, like this:

```
dta clouds.tga /l morf*.tga
```

You're not limited to a single picture for the background, and you're not limited to just two layers. You could overlay a morphing sequence on top of a background, and then layer additional morphs on top of that. For example, this command:

```
dta clouds.tga /l mrfa*.tga /p /l mrfb*.tga /l mrfc*.tga
```

tells DTA to create a flic using the same background image, and to overlay a series of TGA files which have names begining with the string "MRFA". On top of that, it adds another series of TGA files that all begin with the string "MRFB". On the very top, it adds yet another series of TGA files that begin with the string "MRFC". Did you notice the /P switch right after the MRFA*.TGA file specification? It tells DTA to "Ping-Pong" the pictures in that layer (adding those pictures to the animation a second time in reverse order), and will not affect any of the other layers.

Figure 3-14 The foreground composited onto a new background image

"JUST WARP" EFFECTS

DMorf's main function is to morph one picture into another, but that's not all it can do. The mesh-warping technique that it uses to create part of the morphing effect can also be used all on its own to produce some other effects, including some very warped caricatures of people. Remember the scene in the film *PeeWee's Big Adventure*, where the truck driver Large Marge transforms into a horrible monster? That effect was created using Claymation, but you can achieve some similar effects just by warping images.

If you turn on the Just Warp setting in the Morphing Switches menu panel, then DMorf will still use the control meshes from both picture windows, but instead of warping both pictures and blending the results to produce output frames, it will create the frames from just the warped versions of the picture in the first window. Two obvious uses for this technique are to create caricatures, as already mentioned, and to move objects around. Maybe you can discover some others.

Caricatures

Caricatures—humorous pictures that exaggerate the features—are a fun way to tease your friends. And if your boss decides not to give you a raise this year;

or you've just been cheated out of a deserved promotion by the office toady, or your girlfriend or boyfriend dumps you for your best buddy; they're a way to get a nice bit of of nonviolent revenge. DMorf's warping function allows you to stretch a picture every which way, as if it were printed on a rubber sheet. That makes it perfect for making your friends and enemies look stupid. Just as *Spy* magazine used a similar program to stretch Bill Clinton's nose to Pinocchio-like proportions for the cover of their May 1993 issue, you can use DMorf to distort your enemy's picture any way you like.

Let's have a bit of fun with this capability by modifying the image of yours truly, shown in Figure 3-15.

Load the picture into DMorf:

```
dmorf dave.tga
```

Because you only specified one picture file, DMorf will display this picture in both morphing windows. Build a control mesh for the picture on the left, just like you did in Chapter 2. When it's done, copy that mesh into the window on the right, using the 1→2 button. Now have some fun with the mesh on the right. Move the control points around so that instead of matching the picture, the mesh's curves follow more ridiculous paths. Stretch out the cheeks, raise the eyebrows, expand the nose. You'll end up with a screen that looks much like Figure 3-16.

Make sure that the Just Warp setting (which is in the Settings dialog) is switched on, and change the number in the Frames number box (also in the

Figure 3-15 The author, unmodified

Settings dialog box) to 1. Click on the Go button, and let DMorf do its work. You'll end up with a new, warped picture like the one shown in Figure 3-17.

If the object of your caricature could get you fired, it might be a real good idea to enjoy your revenge in private.

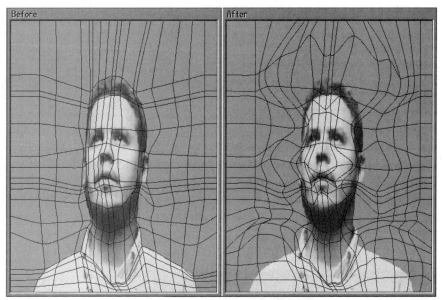

Figure 3-16 Control mesh for the caricature

Figure 3-17 The author, more warped than usual

Moving Objects

Let's say that you've created an image of a rocket ship using a ray-tracing program like POV-Ray. You'd like to make the rocket ship fly across the screen, but you don't feel like taking the time to generate the extra animation frames. DMorf can crank out the output frames quite a bit faster. Start by loading the picture in Figure 3-18, ROCKET.TGA, into DMorf.

Build a mesh for the rocket. Because we don't actually need to warp the rocket's shape, it should be a simple mesh, containing four control points in a rectangle around the rocket. Copy that mesh over to the window on the right (using the 1→2 button), and move the corners of the rectangle to new locations on the screen, as in Figure 3-19.

We're not morphing, so make sure that the Just Warp setting (you'll find the check box in the Settings dialog box) is on. We don't want the rocket's shape to be distorted, so make sure that Spline Mesh and Spline Intervals settings are off. Click on the Go button, and DMorf will produce the sequence of frames shown in Figure 3-20 (on page 62). These pictures will not look as nice as they would if each one had been ray-traced, but it's quicker and easier to set up.

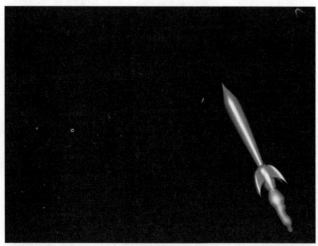

Figure 3-18 The rocket

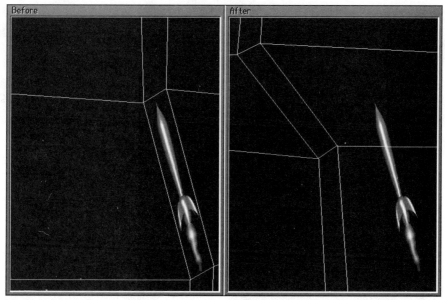

Figure 3-19 Mesh for the rocket in flight

SYMMETRIC MORPHS

Symmetric morphs are a special class of morph, where instead of morphing from one distinct picture to another, you morph one picture into a mirror image of itself. The main uses for this technique are to change the orientation of a person or object, or to turn two people into each other.

To create a symmetric morph, you need to start with just a single picture, not two. This picture must be symmetrical. That means that the features on the left side of the picture must be similar to the features on the right side of the picture. A human head that's facing the camera or turned just a bit to the left or right is symmetrical: there's an ear on one side, and an ear on the other; an eye on one side and another eye on the other side. A profile view of a human head is not symmetrical. For purposes of this exercise, we'll use the DSL.TGA picture created in the section titled "The Background Problem" earlier in this chapter. Load the picture into DMorf by typing:

```
dmorf dsl.tga
```

Figure 3-20 Rocket in flight

Build a control mesh like you did in Chapter 2, except don't bother with the mesh in the window on the right. The mesh must be horizontally symmetrical. If the control point that's two from the left and three from the top is on a particular feature, like the tip of the left ear, then the other control point that's two from the right and three from the top must be on a matching feature on the opposite side of the picture, like the tip of the right ear. Figure 3-21 shows a symmetric control mesh for DSL.TGA.

Figure 3-21 A symmetric mesh

Once you have a symmetric mesh for your before picture, you've done the tough work. You'll still need an after picture and a mirrored mesh, but you can create these pretty easily. To create the after picture, follow these steps:

1. Make sure that the Select option box (on the bottom-right corner of DMorf's main screen) is set to After, and then click on the Edit button on the main menu panel. Because there is no picture number two, DMorf will load in a copy of the first picture instead.

2. On the Edit screen, click the FlipH button. DMorf will flip the picture over horizontally, creating a mirror image of the original picture.

Figure 3-22 Mirror images

3. Click on the SaveAs button. At the Filename prompt type in a new name for this new picture (let's call it DSR.TGA) and press (ENTER).

4. Click on the Main button to return to DMorf's main screen.

To create a mesh for this after picture, follow these steps:

1. Click on the 1→2 button on the main menu panel. DMorf will copy the mesh that you've been working on into the second window.

2. Click on the FlipH button. DMorf will flip the new mesh horizontally, just as it did the picture.

Now we've got a complete setup for a symmetric morph. Figure 3-22 shows the picture windows with their mirror-image pictures and meshes.

Use SaveAs on the main menu panel to save your work so far, and click on Go to process your morph. You'll end up with a sequence that looks like Figure 3-23.

STRINGING MULTIPLE MORPHS TOGETHER

Morphing from one image to another is fun, but the novelty wears off. You can spice things up by morphing a series of pictures. First, morph between the first and second pictures. Then morph from the second picture to a third, and from the third to a fourth. When you're about morphed out, do one more from the final picture back to the first. Make sure to save each series of TGA files under a different filename prefix (using the Output Prefix text box in the Pictures dialog box).

When you've generated all of your TGA output files, it's time to crunch them all into a single flic using DTA. DTA allows you to type as many file

Figure 3-23 A symmetric morph

specifications as you can fit on a command line, so the command should look something like this:

```
dta pict1.tga mrfa*.tga pict2.tga mrfb*.tga pict3.tga mrfc*.tga pict4.tga mrfd*.tga
```

OUTPUT TO VIDEO

When you've spent a lot of time building morphs, and you've shown them off to everybody in the house and to all of your friends who just happen to have PC-compatible computers with VGA monitors, what's left to do? Create a video of your morph sequences, and force all of your other friends to watch! Video output is also extremely useful if you want to make any money off of your animation adventures. Television studios can't do anything with a floppy disk; they require video.

The Way Pros Do It

If money is burning a hole in your pocket, a great way to spend it is on a frame-accurate video tape recorder or a laserdisc recorder. They usually cost $20,000 or more just for the recorder. The extras, which include a Truevision Targa+ graphics board and an animation controller, will cost you even more. However, recording 24-bit images one frame at a time is the very best way to create video from computer graphics.

The Cheap Way

If, like most people, you can't afford a frame-accurate VCR, there's another way. A number of boards and boxes are available (for a lot less money) that

let you pipe the graphics from your computer screen to a regular VCR. These are called NTSC converters.

One such device is called the Presenter+. It costs about $429 at the time of this writing. The Presenter+ is a little box that you can plug into your PC's VGA connecter. An RCA cable (or an SVHS connector) goes out to your VCR. One more cable goes to your monitor. Just run a program that comes with the box to reset the timing on your VGA board, and everything that displays on your monitor at 640 x 480 pixels or less can be displayed on your TV or recorded with your VCR.

SUMMARY

This chapter covered a lot of ground. You learned where to look for just the right picture for the morph that you want to create. You discovered how you can get your morphs to run faster, and how to deal with some of the problems you might encounter. You learned some design tricks, such as lighting and shadow, warping, chaining morphs together, and building symmetric morphs. You've even seen how to store the results on video for posterity, as well as for your viewing pleasure.

Now that you are familiar with the morphing process and enhancement techniques, you should familiarize yourself with the bundled applications. With these advanced skills, you can use the full power of the programs included with this book to create sophisticated, uniquely expressive morphs.

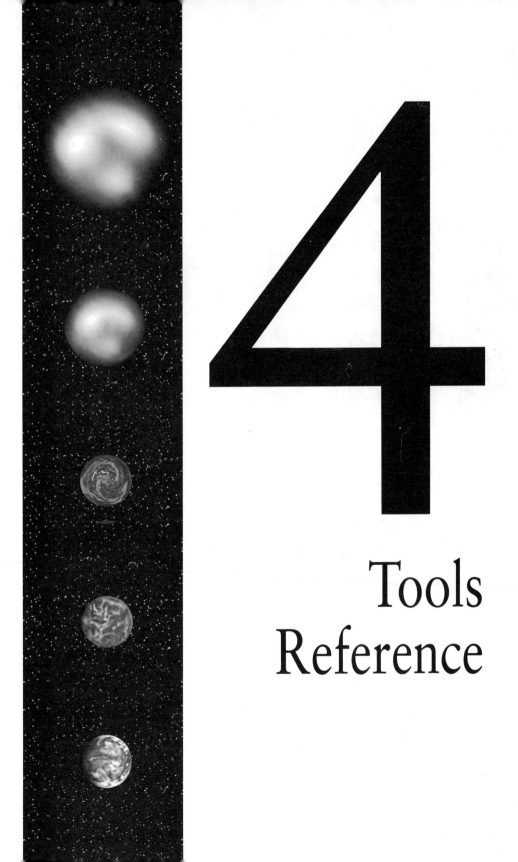

4

Tools
Reference

CHAPTER 4

Tools Reference

Y ou've learned how to build a basic morph and how to personal-
ize it with some special tricks. Now, learn all there is to know
about the morphing tools included with this book, so that you
can use them effectively to create your own even more interesting and outrageous morphs!

The diskettes supplied with this book provide all the tools you need to create and display animations of morph sequences. If you've installed the disks
according to the instructions at the beginning of the book, you will find four
tools in your C:\MORPHING\TOOLS directory:

◆ DMorf (Dave's Morphing Program), which you can use to design
and build your morph sequences

◆ DTA (Dave's TGA Animator), which joins the separate frames of
your morphs into flic animation files

◆ FLISPEED, which lets you change the speed setting in an existing
flic animation file

◆ Trilobyte Play, which will display those flics on your VGA or
SVGA monitor

In this chapter we'll cover each of these programs in detail, revealing all of
the options and features of DMorf, DTA, and FLISPEED, and all of the
important features of Play.

Examples and details in this chapter are aimed at people who are using a regular MS-DOS command line. If you want to run from Microsoft Windows or IBM's OS/2, for convenience or to gain access to more memory, you'll first have to open up a full-screen DOS window. In Windows, click on the MS-DOS icon. In OS/2, click on the Full-Screen DOS icon. The Windows or OS/2 Presentation Manager display will be replaced by a DOS prompt. From here on in, everything will work the the same as if you were running from DOS.

If you haven't already, be sure to follow the special Windows and OS/2 setup instructions in the "Installation" section at the beginning of the book.

DMORF

DMorf is the tool used to edit the morphing control meshes and to generate morphing sequences. In this section we'll discuss all of the different screens, settings, and commands that you'll find in DMorf. For information on creating a morphing control mesh, see Chapter 2.

Many commercial morphing packages are now available, either at software stores or through mail order, including Blackbelt Systems' WinImages:Morph, Gryphon Morph, and North Coast Software's PhotoMorph. Unlike DMorf, these are all real Microsoft Windows applications. They offer such conveniences as multiple overlapping windows and color image display. Of these three, WinImages:Morph appears to be the most sophisticated, with a grab bag of features missing from DMorf, like the capability to morph between animation sequences. The cost of these morphing programs ranges from $149 to $199.

Make sure that DMORF.EXE, DPMI16BI.OVL, and RTM.EXE are all either in your current directory or in a directory that's in your DOS path. If any one of these files is missing, DMorf will not work. The first time you use DMorf, if you get a strange error message about an unsupported chipset, you'll also need DPMIINST.EXE.

There are two different versions of the DMorf program included with this book: DMORF.EXE and DMORFNC.EXE. If your PC does not have a math coprocessor chip, and your main processor is a 286, 386, or 486SX, then you should use DMORFNC.EXE instead of DMORF.EXE. The standard version of the program would work fine, but this version will run much more quickly on systems lacking a floating-point unit. If you'd rather not have to remember to type DMORFNC instead of DMORF, then you should replace DMORF.EXE with DMORFNC.EXE. First, switch to the directory that contains the morphing tools; then delete the original DMORF.EXE; then rename DMORFNC.EXE. These commands will do that for you:

```
cd\morphing\tools
del dmorf.exe
rename dmorfnc.exe dmorf.exe
```

Shareware Information

DMorf is a shareware program that may be freely distributed in unmodified form for evaluation purposes. If you use it frequently, you are requested to pay a registration fee of $35. To register, send the fee to the program's author, David K. Mason, P.O. Box 181015, Boston, MA 02118.

Command-Line Syntax

The simplest way to start up DMorf is just to type

```
dmorf
```

DMorf displays its main screen with no pictures loaded, and with a default mesh containing four corner points. (You won't see the points because they're at the corners around the pictures. All you'll see is a red border on the top, bottom, and sides of each picture.) You can also load the pictures that you want to morph at the same time by typing the filenames as parameters to the DMorf command. You can try this with a couple of files on the included disk. Switch to the MORPHING\CHAP4 directory and type

```
dmorf before.tga after.tga
```

Or you can load a mesh file. A mesh file called TEST.MSH is provided so that you can test this option. From the MORPHING\CHAP4 directory, type

```
dmorf test.msh
```

You could even do both actions at once if you want to load a mesh with a different set of pictures, or the same pictures in a different order:

```
dmorf before after test.msh
```

If, as in the last example, you type any filenames without an extension, DMorf will assume that the files are Targa (TGA) format picture files, so always remember to include the .MSH extension when you want to load a mesh file. If you're morphing GIF-format picture files, remember to include the .GIF extension. DMorf also allows several switches on the command line. A switch is a parameter, which begins with a slash (/) or a dash (-), and tells DMorf to operate in away other than the default manner.

By default, DMorf will try to operate in a Super VGA graphics mode, 640 x 480 in 256 colors, but will drop to 16 colors if your graphics card or VESA graphics driver doesn't support that mode. You can force DMorf to use the 16-color mode even if your graphics card supports the 256-color mode by appending the /NOSVGA parameter to the command line. At the MORPHING\CHAP4 prompt, type:

```
dmorf test.msh /nosvga
```

If your graphics card and monitor support a higher VESA 256-color resolution, you can make DMorf use that resolution with another switch. To force DMorf to use 800 x 600 x 256 mode, add the /800 switch. To force it into 1024 x 768 x 256 mode, add the /1024 switch.

> **Warning:** Before you select one of these resolution options, make sure your monitor supports the mode. If your graphics board supports it but the monitor doesn't, you could damage your monitor!

By default, DMorf uses as little memory as possible. In order to morph at all, it has to create one huge picture buffer, allocating four bytes for each pixel, but it avoids using a whole lot more than that by swapping some intermediate versions of pictures to disk, and by rereading each source picture once for every new picture that it creates. This extra disk access adds significantly to the time that it takes to morph. If you have plenty of memory available, then add the /PRELOAD switch to the command line to make DMorf store the source pictures and temporary pictures in memory all of the time. DMorf will use much more of your memory, and operate much more quickly.

Without /PRELOAD, DMorf uses 256,000 bytes for that one large image buffer, if you're morphing 320 x 200 pictures. If you do use /PRELOAD, it will use up to 1,280,000. With 640 x 480 pictures, those numbers would be 1,228,000 and 6,144,000. If you try to use /PRELOAD and you don't have enough memory to preload the pictures, DMorf will not be able to run.

DMorf only knows how to use extended (XMS) memory. It can't handle memory that's allocated as expanded (EMS) memory or as a cache. If you've got a limited amount of memory (4MB, for example), you're better off not using a cache at all and letting DMorf use it. If you have other applications that require cache, you should probably have multiple sets of AUTOEXEC.BAT and CONFIG.SYS files. If you have MS-DOS 6, you can create a menu of alternative sections in your configuration files, making it much easier to fine-tune your environment for different applications that have special needs. Other programs, like the shareware application Dyna-Boot, also support this.

One last command-line switch is /GO. Use this switch along with the name of a mesh file, and DMorf will generate the morph sequence without any intervention, exiting to DOS when it's done. This makes it easy to build DOS batch files for unattended morphing. For some examples of morphing with batch files, see Chapter 5. Each of the morphing examples in that chapter includes a batch program.

The DMorf Screen

When you start DMorf, you'll see a screen that looks like Figure 4-1. It's broken up into several different windows: two large windows to hold the pictures that you're morphing, and several smaller panels that contain buttons and other GUI widgets for controlling DMorf.

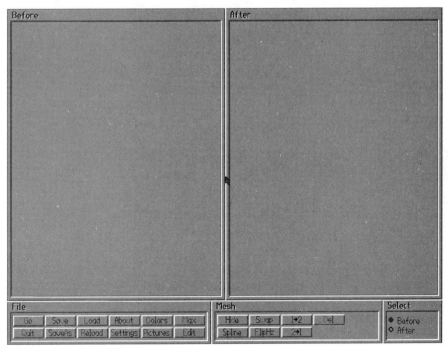

Figure 4-1 DMorf's main screen

The GUI Controls

See all of those buttons, check boxes, and other assorted gizmos in the windows at the bottom of the screen? These are the graphic user interface control objects, known collectively as *widgets,* which you can use to tell DMorf what to do. There are five types of widgets: buttons, check boxes, radio buttons, text boxes, and number boxes. There are three ways to activate a widget: you can click the mouse button while the mouse cursor is pointing at it, type the letter that's highlighted in its label, or move the highlighted selection box to the control using the (TAB) and (SHIFT)-(TAB) keys and then pressing the (SPACE) key.

Buttons

Buttons function as commands. Click the mouse button on a button, or type the letter that's highlighted in its label, and DMorf will perform an action. Figure 4-2 shows two sample button controls.

Figure 4-2 DMorf buttons

Check Boxes

Check boxes control on-off settings. If there's an X in the box to the left of the label, then the setting is on. Otherwise it's off. If you click on either the check box or its label, you'll toggle the setting on and off. Figure 4-3 shows some sample check box controls.

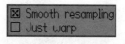

Figure 4-3 DMorf check boxes

Radio Buttons

Radio buttons control settings much like check boxes do, but instead of each one representing an independent on-off setting, radio buttons come in connected groups and represent mutually exclusive options. If you turn one radio button on, any others in the group are automatically turned off. Figure 4-4 shows a sample group of radio button controls.

Figure 4-4 DMorf radio buttons

Number Boxes

Number boxes hold numeric settings. If you click the mouse button while the mouse cursor is pointing at the little button marked with a minus sign, it will lower the number by some preset increment. If you click on the little button marked with a plus sign, it will increase the number by that same increment. If you click on the box containing the number, or type the letter highlighted in the label, DMorf will clear the number in the box, replace it with a text cursor, and allow you to type in a new value. Figure 4-5 displays a sample number box control.

Figure 4-5 DMorf number boxes

Text Boxes

Text boxes hold text string settings. If you click on a text box, DMorf will clear the text, replace it with a text cursor, and allow you to type a new string. Figure 4-6 shows a sample text box.

Figure 4-6 DMorf text boxes

Menus on the Main Screen

The bottom portion of the DMorf screen has three sets of widgets to choose from: File, Mesh, and Select. An explanation of what these widgets do or what they're used for follows.

The File menu panel, displayed in Figure 4-7, is found in the lower-left corner of DMorf's main screen. It is a collection of button widgets for saving and

Figure 4-7 DMorf's file menu panel

loading mesh files, displaying copyright information, switching to other screens, and displaying dialog boxes.

◆ **Go:** Causes DMorf to start morphing or warping.

◆ **Quit:** Exits DMorf. The (ESC) key does the same thing.

◆ **Save:** If you have already saved or loaded a mesh file, this button will save your meshes and settings to that same filename. If not, DMorf will prompt you for a filename first.

◆ **SaveAs:** Prompts you for a new filename and then saves your meshes and settings to that file.

◆ **Load:** Prompts you for the name of an existing control file and then reads it from the disk.

◆ **Reload:** If you have saved or loaded a mesh file already, this button re-reads it from the disk without prompting you for a filename. If not, it behaves just like the Load button.

◆ **About:** Displays a window containing program version and copyright information.

◆ **Settings:** Displays the Settings dialog (described later), which lets you change a variety of morphing parameters.

◆ **Colors:** Displays the Screen Colors dialog (described later). This allows you to modify the colors that DMorf uses to display meshes and represent transparency, and to modify the brightness of the grayscale that DMorf uses to display pictures.

◆ **Pictures:** Displays the Pictures dialog (described later), which allows you to change the picture files that you're morphing and to change the format and name of output files.

◆ **Max:** Switches to a maximized screen, which displays just one of the images and its mesh about twice as large as in the regular view.

This gives much finer control over the mesh points. When you select this button, DMorf will maximize whichever picture is currently specified in the Select option panel.

◆ **Edit:** Switches to an Edit screen, which displays a larger view of one of the pictures and allows you to modify the transparency values of areas or individual pixels. DMorf will edit whichever picture is selected in the Select option panel.

The Mesh menu panel, just to the right of the File menu on the main screen, is displayed in Figure 4-8. It is a collection of buttons that help you manipulate your morphing meshes.

◆ **Hide:** Hides your control mesh temporarily, so that you can see your whole pictures. After you click on this button, keep the mouse button pressed until you're finished looking at the mesh-less pictures.

◆ **Splines:** Gives you a preview of what the splines for the current mesh points would look like. If you're using the Spline Meshes mode (explained later), use this button once in a while to make sure the splines aren't going wacky. After you click on this button, keep the mouse button pressed until you're finished looking at the splines. You won't need to use this button at all if the Spline Always setting (in the Settings dialog) is turned on.

◆ **Swap:** Swaps the meshes between the two windows.

◆ **FlipHz:** Horizontally flips the mesh specified in the Select option panel.

◆ **1→2:** Copies the mesh from the Before window into the After window.

◆ **2→1:** Copies the mesh from the After window into the Before window.

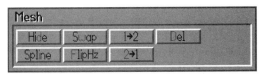

Figure 4-8 DMorf's mesh menu panel

Figure 4-9 DMorf's select option panel

◆◆ **Del:** Lets you delete a line from your meshes. After you click on this button, move the mouse cursor to the border around one of the input pictures near the line that you want to delete, and press the mouse button again. If the cursor is in the top or bottom border, DMorf will delete a vertical line. If the cursor is in one of the side borders, DMorf will delete a horizontal line.

The Select option panel, located in the bottom-right corner of the main screen's menu area, is shown in Figure 4-9. It contains a pair of radio buttons that you can use to choose which of the two pictures displayed on the screen should be affected by some of the other controls on the main screen's menu panels. Buttons affected are Max, Edit, and FlipHZ.

The Max Screen

Sometimes the little picture windows in DMorf's main screen are just too small to either display your pictures in enough detail for you to create a good control mesh, or to give you tight enough control over the mesh vertices. When you click the mouse on the Max button, DMorf switches to the Maxi screen (shown in Figure 4-10), which uses almost the full screen to display one of the pictures and its control mesh. To make room, there are only six button widgets on a Max screen.

◆◆ **Other:** Switches to the Max view for the other picture.

◆◆ **ZoomIn:** Zooms in on a portion of the screen if the maximized view still isn't big enough for you to manipulate your mesh the way you want. After you select this button, move the cursor to one corner of a rectangular area that you're interested in. Press the button again and move the cursor to the opposite corner of the rectangle. Release the button, and DMorf will display just the portion of the picture and mesh that show in the rectangle. In this modified view (displayed in Figure 4-11) you can still manipulate mesh vertices, but you won't be able to add new lines to a mesh. The only new button at the bottom of the screen is ZoomOut, which will take you back to the regular Max screen.

◆ **Main:** Leaves the max screen and returns to the Main Screen.

◆ **Colors:** Pops up the Screen Colors dialog.

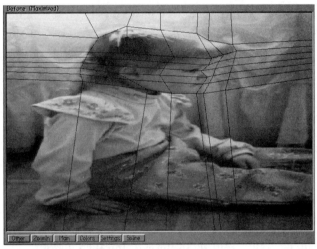

Figure 4-10 DMorf's Max Screen

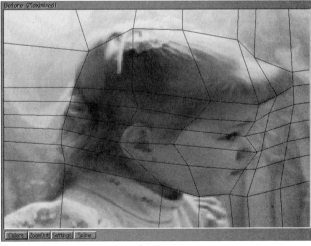

Figure 4-11 A zoomed Max screen

◆ **Settings:** Pops up the Settings dialog.

◆ **Spline:** Displays the curves that correspond to this picture's control mesh.

The Edit Screen

Backgrounds present a problem in morphing. A control mesh that does a fine job of matching the features in a foreground object usually doesn't match the background objects too, especially if the backgrounds in the two pictures are very different. If you click on the Edit button on the main screen, DMorf switches to an Edit screen, shown in Figure 4-12. In Edit mode, DMorf displays just one of the pictures, without its control mesh, and lets you modify the transparency values for areas in the picture, or for individual pixels. This allows you to mask out troublesome background areas.

To save room, an Edit screen only has a single row of button controls:

◆ **Other:** Switches to the Edit view for the other picture.

◆ **Main:** Leaves Edit mode and returns to the main screen.

◆ **Colors:** Pops up the Screen Colors dialog.

◆ **ZoomIn:** Zooms in on a portion of the screen if the Edit view isn't big enough for you to manipulate the picture the way you want to. After you select this button, move the cursor to one corner of a rectangular area that you're interested in. Press the button again and move the cursor to the opposite corner of that rectangle. Release the button, and DMorf will display just that portion of the picture. In this modified view (displayed in Figure 4-13), the mouse button will behave differently. Instead of selecting rectangular areas of the screen to make transparent, it will change individual pixels that you point at with the mouse cursor. There are also fewer buttons at the bottom of a zoomed Edit screen. The only new button is ZoomOut, which will take you back to the regular Edit screen.

◆ **Save:** Saves the picture to disk after you've made changes to the picture. If the picture you're editing is a TGA file, Save will replace the original file. If it was in another format, Save will create a new file with the same filename but with a new extension of .TGA. It will also modify the filename in the Pictures dialog.

◈ **SaveAs:** If you don't want to replace your original file, use this button instead. You'll be prompted for a new filename, and DMorf will create a brand new TGA file. It will also modify the filename in the Pictures dialog.

Figure 4-12 DMorf's Edit screen

Figure 4-13 DMorf's zoomed Edit screen

◆ **FlipHz:** Works like the button of the same name on the main screen's mesh menu, but instead of flipping the mesh, it flips the picture.

◆ **A-Blur:** Performs a blur filter on the picture's alpha channel. This can help you when it's time to composite your modified picture on top of another by making the edges smoother.

◆ **Extend:** This button doesn't do anything now. It's there for future expansion of the Edit screen.

◆ **Key:** This button turns all occurrences of a single color transparent (see the discussion of chroma-keying in Chapter 3). Just click the mouse button while the cursor is pointing at one of the pixels in the picture.

◆ **Tol:** This number box lets you set the tolerance of the Key function. If Tol is set to 0, only identical colors will be affected. If you change it to a higher number, Key will also modify other colors that are nearby in the spectrum.

The Settings Dialog

When you click on the Settings button on one of the other screens, DMorf will pop up the dialog box shown in Figure 4-14. This dialog contains a number of settings that affect how DMorf morphs your pictures. The dialog is divided into two panels. The first, Morph Switches, contains the following check box controls:

◆ **Spline mesh:** When your points are all located where you want them to be, and you tell DMorf to go ahead and morph, DMorf figures out where to move each pixel by drawing spline curves between the vertices. If you turn this control off, it draws straight lines instead. Splined meshes almost always look much better, but you might wish to use lines if (a) your splines go haywire, with curves going every which way, overlapping—sometimes even passing beyond the picture borders—and you don't feel like fixing it, or (b) you don't want something curved when it warps.

◆ **Spline intervals:** DMorf also likes to use a spline function to determine how to space the pixels that fall between the lines in the

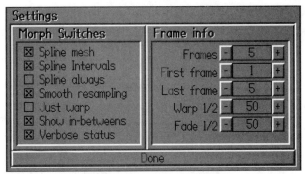

Figure 4-14 DMorf's Settings dialog

meshes. This usually produces nicer output than linear interpolation, but you'll probably want to turn this option off if you're just trying to move an object around instead of warping it.

◆ **Spline always:** Even when set to spline meshes during the morphing process, DMorf displays the meshes on your screen as lines because it's much quicker to display lines on the screen. You can always find out what the splines look like by pressing the Spline button. If you have a fast computer (with a 486DX, -DX2-50, -DX2-66, or Pentium chip), however, turn the Spline Always setting on to make DMorf display splines all the time. If you don't have a math coprocessor, don't even *think* of turning this switch on.

◆ **Smooth resampling:** When this setting is on, DMorf interpolates new pixel values from all source pixels. If you turn this control off, it will operate in Chunky mode instead, and just grab the closest pixel. Chunky mode is only useful for test runs; it's much faster than Smooth mode, but it looks terrible.

◆ **Just warp:** In the default (morph) mode, DMorf maps points from picture 1 toward picture 2, and from 2 toward 1, and cross-fade. In Warp mode, it maps points from 1 toward 2, with no fade. Not too surprisingly, Warp mode takes half the time that morph mode does. You can use Just Warp as a quick and dirty method for moving an object across the screen, or for creating caricatures of people. See Chapter 3, for more details.

◆ **Show in-betweens:** By default, as DMorf performs a morph or warp, it displays each of the warped and blended intermediate frames on the screen. This can be very helpful when you're not sure whether your mesh is going to produce a nice-looking morph. If the intermediate frames look bad, you can always halt the process by pressing the (ESC) key; then change your mesh and morph again. But it takes time to update the screen. If you've got a lot of frames to crank out, you can save a significant chunk of time by turning this setting off.

◆ **Verbose status:** When this setting is on, as it is by default, DMorf displays its progress in detail, showing which frame it's processing and the percentage of that frame that it has completed. If you turn it off, you'll only see which frame is being processed. Turning it off will save you a little bit of time.

The second panel in the Settings dialog is called Frame Info. It contains a set of number box widgets that control animation settings

◆ **Frames:** Tells DMorf how many pictures to create. If you're in Morph mode this represents how many in-between frames to create. In Warp mode, this number includes a fully warped final frame.

◆ **First frame/Last frame:** Specifies a range of output frames to generate if you don't want to create a complete set of TGA files. The output range feature can also be useful if you want to create morphs of animated sequences, but this trick takes more time and effort than the effect warrants. If you absolutely need to morph animated sequences, you'd be better off purchasing BlackBelt Systems' WinImages:Morph program than attempting it in DMorf.

◆ **Warp 1/2:** Changes the rate at which DMorf warps the images. If you set Warp 1/2 to 75, then at 75 percent of the way through the morph, the objects will only be half warped. The warp speeds up at that point so it finishes by the end of the sequence. Using this feature is matter of taste. If you look at the results of your work and feel it would look better if the warp moved at a less constant rate, give Warp 1/2 a try.

◆ **Fade 1/2:** Works the same as Warp 1/2, but affects the rate at which pixel colors are faded from the first picture to the second. It's almost always used along with Warp 1/2. Again, it's a matter of taste whether or not this effect helps. To experiment, try setting Warp 1/2 to 40 percent and Fade 1/2 to 60 percent

The Screen Colors Dialog

When you click on the Colors button on any of DMorf's different screens, DMorf pops up the Screen colors dialog, shown in Figure 4-15. This dialog is a collection of widgets that control the colors that DMorf uses to display things on the screen.

The Mesh panel is a trio of number box controls that let you change the color of the mesh on your screen. This is useful if your meshes don't show up very well because of the shades of grey in your pictures. The default color, <63,0,0>, is bright red. You can change the red, green, and blue components of the color to any value from 0 to 63. (Computer color components usually vary from 0 to 255, but VGA hardware uses only 6 bits per component in 256-color graphics mode.)

The Alpha panel is a set of number boxes that control the color used to display transparent pixels. By default, it's set to <42,42,63>, which is light blue.

The number boxes at the bottom of the dialog labeled File and Disp in the Gamma 1 and Gamma 2 boxes are useful in correcting a problem inherent in most computer monitors. In an ideal world, a pixel with the color value of <10,10,10> should be exactly half as bright as another pixel with the color <20,20,20>. Unfortunately, computer monitors usually don't work that way.

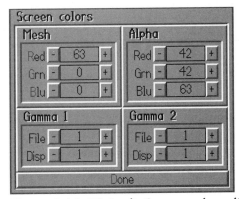

Figure 4-15 DMorf's Screen colors dialog

Instead, there's a lot more variation in brightness right in the middle than there is when you get closer to black or white. So <10,10,10> will probably be less than half as bright as <20,20,20>. The mathematical function that corrects for this phenomenon is called Gamma correction. It remaps all of the colors in a picture so that the brightness curve matches the way your monitor works. All you need is a floating-point number to plug into the Gamma equation. For an uncorrected picture, this number is 1. Most VGA monitors need a value between 1.8 and 2, which makes the picture brighter. Numbers below 1 (but greater than 0!) make a picture darker.

If your pictures look a bit too washed out or murky, it could be because they haven't been Gamma-corrected at all, or they've been corrected to a Gamma value that's incorrect for your monitor. DMorf lets you supply two Gamma values for each picture. The first, Gamma Pict, tells DMorf what Gamma value has already been applied to the picture. Gamma Disp tells DMorf what Gamma value you want it to use when it displays the picture. If both numbers are the same, DMorf won't correct the picture at all.

If your picture is too dark even when it's been corrected to your monitor's correct Gamma setting, you can cheat by putting a higher number in the Gamma Disp number box.

DMorf's Gamma settings only affect how a picture is displayed on your screen. If you want to permanently change your picture file, use DTA's /GA option (described later in this chapter) instead.

The Done button makes the Screen colors dialog go away.

The Pictures Dialog

When you click on the Pictures button on the main screen, DMorf pops up the Pictures dialog, shown in Figure 4-16. This is a collection of widgets that control the source and destination picture files.

The Input files panel is a set of text box widgets that specify which picture files to morph

◈ **Before:** Specifies the picture file that DMorf displays in the Before window on the main screen, and which it uses as a source picture for morphing or as the only picture for Just Warp mode. At present, there's no way to browse from a list of files, but that will probably change in a future version of DMorf.

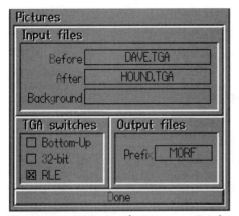

Figure 4-16 DMorf's Pictures Dialog

◆ **After:** Specifies the picture file that DMorf displays in the After window on the main screen, and which it uses as a destination picture for morphing.

◆ **Background:** Specifies the picture file that DMorf places behind output pictures that contain transparent areas.

When DMorf creates TGA files, it begins the output filename with the prefix MORF and adds a frame number to that. In Just Warp mode, DMorf uses WARP as the prefix instead. The Output files panel contains a text box that allows you to change this prefix to any other set of four letters.

The TGA switches panel is a set of check box widgets that control the format of TGA files.

◆ **Bottom-Up:** Tells DMorf whether to create TGA files that begin at the bottom of the screen, or at the top of the screen. Some programs can only read one or the other variety. DTA can read either, but prefers the top-to-bottom variety.

◆ **32-bit:** Tells DMorf whether to create 24-bit or 32-bit TGA files. The only reason you might want to use 32-bit TGA files is if you're planning to do compositing. Some programs can only read 24-bit TGA files. DTA can read either variety.

◆ **RLE:** Tells DMorf whether or not to create run-length encoded (compressed) TGA files. Compressed TGA files are almost always smaller than uncompressed, but some programs can't read them (DTA can).

The Done button makes the Pictures dialog go away.

The DMorf Mesh File Format

This discussion of DMorf wouldn't be complete without a description of the peculiar file format (MSH) that it uses to store control meshes and settings. The majority of readers will never have the need to peer under the covers at the contents of such files. Some of you out there, however, especially programmers who would like to create programs that read or write DMorf's morphing meshes, may find this information useful.

You may also find it quicker to adjust the assorted settings for a morph in a text editor (like MS-DOS's EDIT program) than it would be to load a mesh, display the pictures, and navigate several dialog boxes. You can do this because a MSH file is a regular ASCII text file. A MSH file is broken up into four sections: an identification section, a settings section, and one section each for the two control meshes.

The Identification section, shown in Listing 4-1, contains information about file format and program version information. The first two lines are required; DMorf will not load a mesh file if they're missing. The first tells DMorf that the file is an actual mesh file, and not, say, a letter to the newspaper editor complaining about how Doonesbury was missing from yesterday's comics page. The second line describes the version of the MSH format the file follows. The third line, if you include it, should name the program or process you use to build the mesh. DMorf doesn't do anything with this line, but it can be useful to human beings.

Listing 4-1 Identification section of a MSH file

```
[DMORF MESHFILE]
Version = 7
Program = DMorf Rel. 1.1
```

The Settings section, an example of which is shown in Listing 4-2, contains information corresponding to the settings in DMorf's assortment of dialog boxes. Each line in this section consists of a label identifying the setting, an equal (=) sign, and finally, the value for the setting. The label must contain no spaces. Most of the lines in the Settings section are optional. If you leave them out, DMorf will use default values instead. The only two that you absolutely must include are the first, "[SETTINGS]", because it's the section heading, and the last, which begins "MeshSize", because it tells DMorf how many rows and columns are in the mesh. "[SETTINGS]" must come first, and "MeshSize" must come last, but you can order the rest of the settings in any manner that you wish.

Listing 4-2 Settings section of a MSH file

```
[SETTINGS]
Frames = 5
First = 1
Last = 5
WarpHalf = 50
FadeHalf = 50
JustWarp = False
Smooth = True
Splines = True
SplineAlways = False
SplineIntervals = True
Picture1 =
Picture2 =
MeshColor = <0,0,0>
AlphaColor = <42,42,63>
Gamma1Pict = 1
Gamma1Disp = 1
Gamma2Pict = 1
Gamma2Disp = 1
TGABottomUp = False
32BitTGA = True
TGACompression = True
OutputPrefix = MORF
MeshSize = <6,3>
```

There are two Picture sections, one beginning "[PICTURE 1]" and the other beginning "[PICTURE 2]", shown in Listing 4-3. Each contains the locations for all of a mesh's control points. Each picture section is broken up into smaller groups, separated by a blank line, which contain all of the points for a single row in the mesh. If all of the points for a row don't fit on an 80-character line, then the row is broken up into multiple lines.

Each point consists of a less-than sign (<); followed by a floating-point number representing the horizontal coordinate of the point; a comma (,); another number representing the vertical coordinate for the point, and finally a greater-than sign (>). All numbers fall in the range of 0 through 9999. The 0 represents the left or top edge of a picture, while 9999 represents the right or bottom edge of a picture.

All points on the four edges of a picture must *remain* on the border. This means that all points on the top row of a mesh *must* have a vertical coordinate of 0; all points on the leftmost column *must* have a horizontal coordinate of 0; all points on the bottom row of a mesh *must* have a vertical coordinate of 9999; and all points on the rightmost column *must* have a vertical coordinate of 9999. If not, your morph will almost certainly not work at all. If you try to morph with such a mesh, DMorf will probably abort to the DOS command line with a cryptic runtime error message.

Each horizontal coordinate in a row must be larger than the horizontal coordinate before it. Each vertical coordinate in a column must be larger than the vertical coordinate above it. If you don't follow this rule, your morph may not work at all, and it will look very strange if it does work.

Listing 4-3 Picture sections of a MSH file

```
[PICTURE 1]
<0,0> <1600,0> <3800,0> <5600,0> <8199,0> <9999,0>

<0,5399> <1671.018,3530.612> <3916.449,7102.041> <5718.016,3673.469>
<7989.556,7040.816> <9999,4408.164>

<0,9999> <1600,9999> <3800,9999> <5600,9999> <8199,9999> <9999,9999>

[PICTURE 2]
<0,0> <1600,0> <3800,0> <5600,0> <8199,0> <9999,0>

<0,5399> <4229.765,5244.898> <5926.893,5306.123> <7650.13,5346.939>
<9451.697,5367.347> <9999,5399>

<0,9999> <1600,9999> <3800,9999> <5600,9999> <8199,9999> <9999,9999>
```

This concludes our survey of DMorf's options and features. Now let's move on to DTA, which will turn your morphed output into flics.

DTA

Once you have created a series of picture files, you still need to be able to display them very quickly to achieve the effect of animation. You could use a display program that would load and display each picture sequentially, but that would be far too slow to create an effective illusion of movement. It takes too much time to read a picture from disk and update the whole screen.

DTA (Dave's TGA Animator) assembles all of your pictures in a single flic file, which stores just the differences between the frames in an animation and saves tons of memory and disk space. If you've got enough memory in your PC, a player program can load an entire flic into memory, completely eliminating the disk overhead. It also takes a lot less time to update only a portion of the screen.

Some commercial programs that let you create flics are Autodesk's Animator Pro, Mathematica's Tempra Turbo Animator, and Presidio's PC Animate. The main benefit of such programs is that they allow you to create animations interactively and edit the frames using traditional (and not-so-traditional) painting tools. However, when you're compiling an animation from a large collection of still images created with DMorf or from a rendering program like Polyray or POV-Ray, DTA's command-line interface can save you a lot of time and tedium over loading pictures one at a time with a dialog box. So even if you already have one of these animation packages, you'll probably still want to build your morph flics with DTA.

Shareware Information

DTA is a shareware program that may be freely distributed in unmodified form for evaluation purposes. If you use it frequently, you are requested to pay a registration fee of $35. To register, send the fee to the program's author at the following address: David K. Mason, P.O. Box 181015, Boston, MA 02118.

Preparation

This section contains a number of example command lines that you should try out to get the feel of using DTA. Many examples won't work unless you to have a series of morphed Targa (TGA) files. Let's use DMorf now to build these example files. From the MORPHING\CHAP4 directory, type:

```
dmorf test.msh /go
```

DMorf will load the TEST.MSH file and morph between the pictures BEFORE.TGA and AFTER.TGA. You'll end up with ten new Targa files, named TEST0001.TGA, TEST0002.TGA, and so on, up to TEST0010.TGA. It's not a particularly interesting morph, but it'll be fine for testing DTA .

Creating a Simple Flic

Let's assume you've created a bunch of Targa files and you want to turn them into a flic. The easiest way is to type the DTA command with a wildcard filename, like this:

```
dta *.tga
```

This command causes DTA to go through all the TGA files in the current directory. DTA scans your pictures to figure out which colors they contain, generates a 256-color VGA palette, and then crunches the pictures into a flic file. This only works correctly if the names of your files are in a sequence, like TEST0001.TGA, TEST0002.TGA, TEST0003.TGA, and so forth, because DTA sorts the filenames before processing. If you have any other TGA files in the current directory, they also will be included in the animation, probably in the wrong order. For example, in your \MORPHING\CHAP4 directory, you've got files named BEFORE.TGA, and AFTER.TGA, in addition to the ten other TGA files we built that begin with TEST. BEFORE.TGA and AFTER.TGA would be sorted along with the rest. Because "AFTER" comes first alphabetically, it would go into the flic first. "BEFORE" goes in next, and all of the rest would be piled on at the end.

What if you have other pictures in the current directory and would rather not move them elsewhere? If you were using the previously mentioned example files, you could use a more specific wildcard file specification, like this:

```
dta test*.tga
```

DTA still processes all of the files in your sequence, but it ignores all picture files that do not begin with TEST. You'll probably also want the before and after pictures for your morph included at the beginning and end of your flic, so you should add them to the line as well. In our example, you could type:

```
dta before.tga test*.tga after.tga
```

Because you specified BEFORE.TGA and AFTER.TGA as separate parameters in the correct order, DTA won't sort those filenames in with the rest. AFTER.TGA will appear at the end even though it comes before BEFORE.TGA and all of the TEST*.TGA files in the alphabet. If you don't want to use a wildcard, as in the previous examples, you can specify each of your files by name. They'll be added to your new flic in the order you typed them:

```
dta test0004.tga test0002.tga.tga test0009.tga
```

That gets boring fast if you have a lot of images, so DTA provides one more method of specifying files. With your text editor, you can create a text file containing the names of the pictures that you want to compile into a flic. Let's build one using the DOS full-screen editor. From the \MORPHING\CHAP4 subdirectory, type:

```
edit pics.lst
```

EDIT will open up an empty editing screen, where you can type the names of the picture files. Type:

```
test0005.tga
test0003.tga
test0007.tga
test0001.tga
```

Pull down EDIT's File menu with your mouse and click on the Save menu entry. Pull down the File menu again and click on Exit. Once you've saved the list file, you can tell DTA to process the pictures listed therein by typing the new file's name, preceded by an "@." You just created one called PICS.LST, so from the \MORPHING\CHAP4 you'd type:

```
dta @pics.lst
```

DTA will create a flic using the files listed, in the order that they occur in the file. This is useful if your filename order doesn't match the order in which you want the pictures to be added to your flic. You can include any of the file types listed in the next section. You can't include another list file.

Files That DTA Can Read

DTA can read many kinds of files and convert them into a single flic. The most common true-color format in the PC graphics world is called the Targa (TGA for short) format, and was originally designed by Truevision for use with their Targa graphics boards. TGA files come in 8-, 16-, 24-, and 32-bit versions, compressed and uncompressed. Since this is the only type of image file that DMorf creates, you'll be seeing a lot of them. DTA also reads the following formats:

◆ GIF files—The CompuServe Graphics Interchange Format is the most common format for 256-color pictures. DTA can read both the GIF87a and GIF89a varieties.

◆ IMG files—Stephen Coy's Vivid ray tracer creates this format.

◆ PCX files—Originally designed for ZSOFT's PC Paintbrush program, PCX has developed into a standard graphics file format, supported by many applications. It comes in several varieties, supporting everything from black-and-white pictures, up to 24-bit pictures. DTA can only read the 256-color and 24-bit varieties.

◆ FLI/FLC files—"Flic" animation files. You can use this feature to combine flics into longer flics, or to add frames to a flic. DTA loads them rather slowly, so avoid reading flics if you can.

◆ ANI files—Presidio's PC Animate Plus and 3D Workshop programs create this format.

◆ BMP/DIB files—Microsoft Video for Windows, or any number of other Microsoft Windows graphics programs, create this format.

DTA can also process standard compressed archive files. These are just containers for picture files. Archive formats that DTA supports are

◆ LZH—Haruyasu Yoshizaki's LHA archiving program creates this format. A copy of LHA.EXE must be on your disk, in a directory that's in your DOS path, for DTA to read pictures from these files.

◆ ZIP—PKWare's PKZIP archiving program creates this format. You will have to have a copy of PKUNZIP.EXE installed somewhere in your DOS path for DTA to be able to read these.

◆ ARJ—Robert Jung's ARJ archiving program creates this format. You must have a copy of ARJ.EXE in your DOS path for DTA to be able to read these files.

Command-Line Switches

Sometimes the settings that DTA selects by default won't give you the results you want. You can make DTA operate differently by entering switches on the DTA command line. Every switch begins with a (/) or a dash (-), so that DTA will know it isn't a filename, and is followed by a letter or two letters identifying the switch. When a switch takes an additional parameter, there is no space between the switch letter and the text of the parameter.

Unlike some programs, DTA's switches are not case sensitive. The switch, "/FT" means exactly the same thing as "/ft." In the command-line examples in this section, switches will be presented in lowercase, because that's the way people usually type. In regular text, they're shown in uppercase, so they'll stand out.

Output File Format (/F)

By default, DTA will create a flic animation file from your input pictures. It can also create files in a number of non-animation file formats. Table 4-1 lists all of the formats that DTA can create, and the switches you can use to select them. The palette formats are useful if you want to use the /U (use palette) switch described a little later. The other formats won't help you create animation, but can be very useful if you want to use some of DTA's tricks to create still pictures, or to convert between still file formats.

Output File Name (/O)

If you don't tell it otherwise, DTA will name the new file ANIM.FLI. You could tell it to change the name to SOMETHNG.FLI by using the /O switch, like this:

```
dta *.tga /osomethng
```

You don't have to supply an extension, because DTA will pick one based on the output file format.

Resolution (/R#)

If you don't provide a resolution switch, DTA will create a flic that's 320 pixels across by 200 pixels down. That's the resolution of the original FLI file format

Switch	Output Format
/FG	GIF (CompuServe Graphics Interchange Format)
/FT	TGA (Targa) format
/FM	MAP palette format (used by Fractint and Piclab)
/FC	COL palette format (used by Autodesk Animator)
/FI	Grayscale TIFF (Tagged Image File Format)
/FP	PCX (used by PC Paintbrush and other packages)

Table 4-1 Format switches

from Autodesk Animator. It's also the only resolution supported by a number of flic players, such as AAPLAY, AADEMO, and QUICKFLI.

DTA will allow you to create a flic with a different resolution by typing the /R switch. Table 4-2 lists available resolutions and the switches that you can use to select them.

In addition, you can use /RA to create an FLI file of the same resolution as your TGA files, whatever that might be.

If you use any resolution other than 320 x 200, you must have a flic player that can read it. Trilobyte's Play and Autodesk's WAAPLAY player for Microsoft Windows can both display high-resolution flics if you have a Super VGA monitor.

Speed (/S#)

By default, DTA will put a "speed" value of 0 into your flic file. This tells the flic player to move the frames of your animation to the screen as fast as it possibly can. If that's too fast, you can change the speed using the /S# value.

If you're creating a 320 x 200 flic (the original Autodesk Animator format), then the number you type following the /S# represents a number of 1/70 of a second. So if you type /S5, the screen will be updated no more than 14 times per second.

Switch	Resolution
/R1	320 x 200 (default)
/R2	320 x 240
/R3	320 x 400
/R4	320 x 480
/R5	360 x 480
/R6	640 x 480 (the second most useful resolution)
/R7	640 x 400
/R8	800 x 600
/R10	1024 x 768
/R12	1280 x 1024
/RA	Automatic

Table 4-2 Resolution switches

If you're creating a flic with any resolution other than 320 x 200, the speed value represents a number of milliseconds.

In some cases, the information content (the change per frame) exceeds what your hardware can support. In that case, the speed is governed by the factors such as the speed of data transfer to VGA memory and, when there isn't enough RAM to hold the entire flic, disk access. If disk access is the bottleneck, you can sometimes speed things up by defragmenting your hard disk with a product such as SPEEDISK, which comes with Symantec's Norton Utilities.

If you don't get the speed value correct the first time, there's no need to rebuild your flic from scratch with the correct speed value. Instead use the FLISPEED utility, also included with this book, to modify the speed setting in an existing flic. FLISPEED is described in a bit more detail later in this chapter.

Repeating Frames (/REP#)

The speed setting in a flic decides how long every frame in a flic should remain on the screen. But each flic has only one speed; you can't make one frame stay on the screen longer than the rest. So what do you do if you want to make your morphing flic pause a bit when it's displaying your before and after pictures? Include those pictures in the flic more than once. You can do this by simply typing the names of those pictures several times in a row on the command line. For example:

```
dta before.tga before.tga before.tga test*.tga after.tga after.tga after.tga /s1
```

When DTA builds this flic, it will display the beginning frame and the ending frame four times longer than the in-between frames, adding a nice pausing effect. Of course, it won't work if your flic has a speed setting of 0. When it's set to 0, a player will display the frames in a flic as fast as it possibly can, and the repeated pictures won't stay on the screen any longer than the nonrepeated pictures. So always use a speed value of at least 1 if you're going to repeat any frames.

All that extra typing is a pain in the neck, and it becomes even more of a pain in the neck the more times you want to repeat. So, DTA provides a shortcut method for repeating a frame without actually having to type the filename more than once: the /REP# switch. Instead of repeating the filename, type each filename once, but add /REP# and the number of times to repeat it. The preceding command line above could be shortened to:

```
dta before.tga /rep2 test*.tga after.tga /rep2
```

Color Selection

In a true-color image (like the pictures you create in DMorf), each pixel's color is made up of three numbers, which represent red, green, and blue. Each of these values can be any number from 0 and 255. So there are 16,777,216 possible colors. One 320 x 200 picture might contain as many as 64,000 different colors. A 640 x 480 picture could contain 307,200 different colors.

Unfortunately, VGA monitors can only display 256 colors on the screen at a time, so DTA must pick 256 colors that approximate all of the colors in all of the images. To do this, DTA uses a gimmick called Octree Quantization, a quick and low-memory-overhead alternative to such common color-reduction methods as Popularity and Median-Cut. DTA scans each of your pictures to find out what colors they contain, and then selects the best 256 to use in the flic. This method produces the best palette that DTA is capable of creating.

Grayscale Palettes (/G and /G32)

If you use the /G switch, DTA will create a palette of 64 shades of gray instead of using color. If you use the /G32 switch, DTA will use a palette of 32 shades of gray. This is probably only useful if you're going to be displaying your animations on a laptop with a grayscale display. Many laptops can only display 32 shades. DTA can create grayscale flics much more quickly than it can if it uses color, because there's no need to scan all of the pictures first or search through a tree to pick colors.

3/3/2 Palette (/332)

If you select the /332 switch, DTA will use a palette containing combinations of eight shades of red, eight shades of green, and four shades of blue. (It's called a 3/3/2 palette because that's how many bits are used for each color component.) Animations that use this palette look rather dreadful, but DTA can create them very quickly.

External Palette (/U)

If you have a palette file created outside of DTA, or with DTA, in the COL (Autodesk Animator) or MAP (PICLAB/FRACTINT) format, then you can tell DTA to use that palette with the /U switch, like this:

```
dta *.tga /uneon.map
```

Instead of generating its own palette based on the colors in the image, DTA will use the set of colors defined in the palette file NEON.MAP, a palette file that's included with the Stone Soup Group's FRACTINT program. (See Waite

Group Press titles *Fractal Creations,* by Tim Wegner and Mark Peterson, *Fractals for Windows,* and *Image Lab,* by Tim Wegner, for more information, about FRACTINT.)

Original Palette (/NM)

If you're starting with a collection of 256-color GIF or PCX files that already have a palette, then you can use the /NM switch to tell DTA not to create a new palette at all. DTA will use the palette of the first picture in the group and won't remap any of the colors. Don't use this trick if your 256-color images contain different palettes, unless you really enjoy digital noise.

Dithering

After DTA has reduced the number of colors in an image, it often won't look as good as the original. When some small detail of your picture has an "unpopular" color (meaning, that color doesn't appear very much in the picture), it will often end up mapped to the wrong color. For example, imagine you create a picture containing one yellow banana in a bowl of oranges on a brown table in the middle of a tan room. All of these colors are fairly close to each other in the spectrum, and when DTA decides which shades in the yellow/orange/tan area to use, it is going to pick the more popular shades. Chances are, you are going to end up with an orange, brown, or tan banana.

Groups of different but similar colors get reduced to a single color, so any areas in your pictures containing a smooth gradation from one color to another will end up as several bands of discrete colors, as you can see in Figure 4-17.

We can use a technique called *dithering* to trick your eye into seeing more colors than are actually there. The way it works is that while each individual pixel might contain an incorrect color, a group of pixels will approximate the right colors. DTA provides several methods of dithering your picture: Floyd-Steinberg, Sierra-Lite, Ordered, and Random noise.

Floyd-Steinberg and Sierra-Lite (/DF and /DS)

Floyd-Steinberg (/DF) and Sierra-Lite (/DS) are both *error-diffusion* dithering methods, and both work in the following way. Whenever a perfect match can not be made between an input color and an output color, DTA takes the following steps:

1. Calculates the difference, in red/green/blue values, between the two colors (the *error*).

2. Divides the error up into smaller chunks.

Figure 4-17 *Color banding*

3. Subtracts the error chunks from the colors of some of the other pixels in the neighborhood.

DTA then uses the modified colors to select the output colors for those pixels. All of the pixels end up with wrong colors, but your eye will be fooled into seeing the correct shades.

The only difference between F-S and S-L dithering is how many pixels receive part of the error. F-S modifies four pixels, and S-L modifies two.

Of all the dithering methods that DTA supplies, these error-diffusion techniques tend to produce the nicest-looking output (see Figure 4-18). On the other hand, error-diffusion doesn't work very well with flic compression. Even if there are only minor differences between the TGA files for two frames in an animation, error-diffusion dithering can result in large differences in the flic frames...and very large and slowly-playing flics. So only use /DF and /DS if you've got plenty of disk space and a fast computer.

Ordered Dithering (/DO#)

Ordered dithering works by imposing a pattern on a picture. It adds or subtracts numbers to the colors in the input picture based on a pattern table. It can be described as viewing your flic through a screen door.

The number that you can enter along with the /DO# switch represents the "strength" of the pattern, or how big the numbers that are used to modify the colors can be. A switch of /DO1 adds a very light pattern to your pictures. A

Figure 4-18 Sample error-diffusion dither

switch of /DO7 can make your animation look a lot like a bad tapestry, as shown in Figure 4-19.

Ordered dithering won't cause the size of your flic to expand nearly as much as error-diffusion dithering. That's because the numbers it uses to filter your images will always be the same from one frame to another. But it will still be larger than a nondithered flic.

Figure 4-19 Sample ordered dither

Random Noise Dithering (/DR#)

Random noise dithering works a lot like ordered dithering, except instead of using a pattern, it just modifies the colors in your picture with numbers that it makes up as it goes along.

Instead of making your pictures look like needlepoint, the random noise dither adds a grainy look. The pixel colors are less accurate than with the previous dithering methods, but it usually looks nicer than an ordered dither. Take a look at Figure 4-20 for an example.

The "random" numbers that DTA filters your pictures with aren't really random. They'll stay the same from one frame to the next, so you won't get the "ballooning FLI" effect. Dithered regions remain fixed from frame to frame.

Picture Scaling (/SC)

When you build a flic from pictures that are smaller than the screen size, DTA will center them on the screen and fill the rest of the screen with a black border. Figure 4-21 shows a 100 x 100 picture displayed on a 320 x 200 screen.

Sometimes this will look just fine, but other times you'll want to use up a bit more of the screen's real estate. You can use the /SC switch to resize the pictures to fill the whole screen:

```
dta small.tga /sc
```

DTA will scale the pictures to the screen's dimensions (320 x 200 if you don't use the /R switch). Take a look at Figure 4-22 for the result.

Figure 4-20 Sample random noise dither

Figure 4-21 No scaling

Figure 4-22 Scaling with /SC

Sometimes you'll want to resize the picture, but not to the exact dimensions of the screen. In the current example, scaling a 100 x 100 picture to 320 x 200 warps the picture badly. DTA allows you to supply it with a specific size:

```
dta small.tga /sc200,200
```

Now DTA will scale to 200 x 200 instead of 320 x 200. See Figure 4-23.

Figure 4-23 Scaling with /SC200,200

Picture Clipping (/CL)

When you build a flic from pictures that are larger than the screen size, DTA will clip pixels off of the bottom and right ends of the picture in order to make it fit. To make DTA clip those pixels off of the top or the left, use /CL and the number of pixels to clip off, as in:

```
dta test*.tga /cl100,100
```

If you want just a portion of your picture to show up on the screen, you can supply four numbers to the /CL option:

```
dta test*.tga /cl100,50,150,120
```

This results in a 150 x 120 pixel piece being clipped out of each picture and placed in the middle of the screen area. The top-left corner of the little window will start with the pixel located 100 pixels from the left of the source picture, and 50 pixels down.

Picture Placement (/ST)

When you have a source picture that's smaller than the flic resolution (because it started that way or because you scaled it or clipped it), DTA will place it in the very center of the output. You can make DTA place it elsewhere with the /ST switch:

```
dta small.tga /st 0,0
```

This causes your small picture to be placed in the top-left corner of the screen when you play the flic, instead of right in the middle.

Frame Averaging (/A# and /T#)

In computer animation generated with a ray tracer, a single frame represents only a single instant in time. In live-action film, a frame represents a short but measurable length of time. You can see the effect of this difference when you press the pause button on a VCR while an object is moving very quickly across the TV screen. You see a blur across the area where the object moves between the one frame and the next. This effect is called *motion blur*. In each frame from a computer animation, though, the object will appear perfectly clear regardless of how much it moves.

For added realism, DTA allows you to get a fake motion blur effect by averaging multiple frames. Just use the /A# switch, along with a number representing a number of frames to average, like this:

```
dta *.tga /a3
```

DTA will create a flic in which every group of three input pictures are combined into a single frame. Of course, this means you'll have to create three times as many pictures. By default (if you use /A# without a number), DTA will average every two frames.

The /T# (trail) option works much like /A#, but starts a new frame from every input picture. The sequence created with /T3 looks like 1-2-3, 2-3-4, 3-4-5, instead of 1-2-3, 4-5-6, 7-8-9.

Frame averaging is almost completely useless for morph output, but you'll be glad the feature's there if you ever do any 3-D rendering.

Multiple Layers (/L)

When you supply DTA with the names of a bunch of picture files, it will add them sequentially to your flic file. With the /L switch, you can cause DTA to put more than one picture into the same output frame. To try this, assume you have two sets of files, XXX001.TGA through XXX005.TGA and YYY001.TGA through YYY005.TGA. For example, you would type:

```
dta xxx*.tga /l yyy*.tga /l zzz*.tga
```

After this command, DTA places the picture from XXX001.TGA into the first output frame. Next it overlays that picture with YYY001.TGA If XXX001.TGA is smaller or equal in size to YYY001.TGA, then it will be completely covered up. If YYY001.TGA is a 32-bit file with alpha information in it (explained in Chapter 3, under "The Background Problem"), then parts of XXX001 will show through the transparent portions of YYY001.TGA in the second frame. The same will happen with XXX002.TGA and YYY002.TGA.

Each set of files is called a *layer* and is separated from the other layers on the command line with the /L switch. You can have as many layers as you can specify on the command line. You can scale (/SC), clip (/CL), Ping-Pong (/P), place (/ST), average (/A), or expand (/X) each layer separately.

The most important use for /L is to composite pictures on top of backgrounds:

```
dta bricks.gif /l before.tga morf*.tga after*.tga /st110,100 /l fence.tga
```

Assuming BRICKS.GIF is a 320 x 200-pixel image of a brick wall, that the pictures in the middle layer are a 100 x 100-pixel morph sequence, and that FENCE.TGA is another 320 x 200-pixel image of a chain-link fence with all of the non-chain pixels transparent, then you'll end up seeing your morph and the brick wall through the fence. The first and last layers have fewer frames than the middle layer, so DTA will repeat BRICKS.TGA and FENCE.TGA for each of the additional frames.

You can also use /L along with /ST to tile animations. Let's assume you've created four low-resolution (160 x 100) morphs and want to display them all simultaneously. This command should do it:

```
dta mrfa* /st0,0 /l mrfb* /st160,0 /l mrfc* /st 0,100 /l mrfd* /st160,100
```

Chroma-Key (/CH, /CT#)

The previous section on multiple layers discussed overlaying pictures that contain transparency on top of other pictures. So how do you make the pixels transparent? You could use DMorf's editing feature, but what if you have a whole bunch of pictures and don't want to take the time? DTA's /CH switch will let you turn all occurrences of a color transparent. Just tell DTA what color in R,G,B format, like this:

```
dta backgrnd.tga /l fore*.tga /ch0,0,0
```

That will make all black pixels in the foreground images transparent.

What if the background isn't all exactly the same shade? Use a color tolerance:

```
dta backgrnd.tga /l fore*.tga /ch255,0,0 /ct20
```

That will make all red pixels, or pixels that are mostly red, transparent.

Skipping Frames (/C#, /K#, /I#)

If you have a large number of frames in an animation project, it can take DTA a long time to process them. DTA must first scan every single picture to build a palette, and then read them all over again when it builds a flic. You can speed things up by using the /C# switch, which instructs DTA to ignore some of the frames while it's building a palette:

```
dta *.tga /c5
```

DTA will then scan only once for every five pictures. Because sequential frames almost always share very similar colors, the palette usually looks just as good. Don't use this feature if each of your colors varies widely from frame to frame. If you use the /C# switch without supplying a number, DTA assumes you mean /C2.

The /K# switch tells DTA not to use some of the frames at all, making your flic shorter. For example, type the following command:

```
dta *.tga /k3
```

DTA will use only one of every three pictures. If you start with 30 TGA files, the resulting flic will contain only 10 frames. If you don't supply a number along with the /K# switch, DTA assumes you mean /K2, and skips every other picture.

You can use both the /C# and /K# parameters:

```
dta *.tga /k2 /c3
```

In this case DTA will skip every other picture, and of the remaining pictures, it will only scan one picture out of three to build the palette. If you start with 12 pictures, only pictures 0 and 6 will be used for palette pictures, and only pictures 0, 2, 4, 6, 8, and 10 will show up in the flic.

If you want to use a specific number of frames rather than a percentage of frames, use /I# instead:

```
dta frames*.tga /i25
```

No matter how many input files there are, DTA will create a 25-frame animation. If there are more than 25 input pictures, the 25 that it uses will be evenly sampled from the files. If there are fewer than 25 input pictures, some of them will be repeated in the flic.

The /K# and /I# switches help out when you want to get a rough idea of how a sequence will look but don't want to wait for DTA to create a full version of the flic. They also come in handy when you discover you've generated too many frames, so your flic is too long. Instead of remorphing with fewer frames, just tell DTA not to use all of them.

Frame Expansion (/X#)

If the motion in your flic looks too jumpy or jerky, it's probably because you didn't render enough frames. The best way to correct the problem is to re-render twice as many frames. If you're in a rush, you can use the /X# switch instead:

```
dta *.tga /x
```

DTA will create a flic containing an extra averaged frame between each pair of regular frames in your flic. If you want more than a single extra frame, add a number after the /X#.

You won't have much use for frame expansion when you're creating your pictures with DMorf, because you can always increase the number of output frames within DMorf. This switch comes in handy, though, when you're creating your frames with a 3-D renderer.

Ping-Pong (/P)

Earlier in the book we talked about looping, which means making sure that the end of a flic is the same as the beginning. This prevents the animation from skipping when a flic player finishes playing it and starts it up again. If you have a nonlooping set of pictures, DTA can fix that by using the Ping-Pong effect. DTA adds each of your pictures to the animation, then it adds each of the frames again to the end in reverse order. If you start out with five frames in the animation, for example, the Ping-Pong flic will insert the pictures in the order 1-2-3-4-5-4-3-2.

3-D (/3D)

The /3D option tells DTA to create a red/blue 3-D effect, the kind that you need those special red-and-blue 3-D glasses to see. Assuming you've got a collection of Targa files labeled LEFT000.TGA, LEFT001.TGA, and so on, which should be used for the image that the left eye sees, and another collection labeled RGHT000.TGA, RGHT001.TGA, and so on, which should be used for the image that the right eye sees, then run DTA with this command line:

```
dta left*.tga rght*.tga /3d /o3d
```

DTA will generate a flic called 3D.FLI. All the images from the "LEFT" series of Targas get displayed in red, and all the "RGHT" pictures get displayed in blue.

Note that you can't use just any combination of pictures to produce a nice 3-D effect. You'll have to generate two sets of pictures, with the camera positions spaced apart from each other. In addition, the points that the cameras are looking at must be separated by the same amount of space as the "eyes." Creating such pictures is beyond the scope of this book.

Creating Targa Files (/NC, /B#)

By default, when DTA creates a Targa file (with /FT) it will compress it using run-length encoding. Unfortunately, not all applications that can read Targas know how to read the compressed ones. In such a case, tell DTA not to compress by using the /NC (no compression) option. DTA's other Targa-related default is to create them using 24-bit color. You can tell it to create 8-bit grayscale Targas with /B8, 16-bit Targas with /B16, or 32-bit Targas with /B32.

That's it for DTA. Now you know how to use DTA to its fullest.

FLISPEED

When you build a flic, you can save a speed setting that a player program uses to decide how long to display each frame. It's frustrating to find out, after waiting for DTA to build a flic, that you used the wrong speed value. You can wait some more while DTA rebuilds the flic for you, or you can use FLISPEED instead. FLISPEED modifies the speed of a flic without going to all the trouble of building it from scratch.

FLISPEED is a command-line utility just like DTA. It takes as its first parameter a flic's filename. By default FLISPEED will put a speed value of 0 into your flic file. This tells the flic player to move the frames of your animation to the screen as fast as it possibly can. This is usually much too fast, so add the /S (speed) parameter to insert a larger number. If it's a 320 x 200 flic (the original Autodesk Animator format), the number you type following the /S represents a number of 1/70 of a second. If you type /S5, for example, the screen will be updated no more than 14 times per second. From the MORPHING\CHAP4 subdirectory type

```
flispeed test.fli /s4
```

FLISPEED will change the speed value in the flic's header area without touching any other part of the flic. It will *not* change the file's date and time when it makes this change.

TRILOBYTE PLAY

Once you've built all of your Targa files with DMorf and translated them into a flic with DTA, you still haven't seen anything move. For that, you need the Play program, from Trilobyte. Play can load even large flics completely into memory and display them *fast*.

Commercial equivalents to this program don't really exist at all, except as components of a larger animation package. Both Autodesk's Animator Pro and Presidio's PC Animate include command-line viewers that users can include with their finished flics. Mathematica's Tempra Turbo Animator requires you either to display a flic inside of the animation program, or to build a script file with Media Author, an add-on animation sequencing program.

Play can display low-resolution (320 x 200) flics on any VGA display, or higher-resolution (640 x 480) flics on pretty much any Super VGA display. For resolutions higher than 640 x 480, you must have a VESA-compatible Super VGA or VESA driver.

Shareware Information

Play is not a free program. If you find it useful and continue using it after you've tried it out, you must make a registration payment of $39.00 to Trilobyte, P.O. Box 1412, Jacksonville, OR 97530.

Running PLAY

To run Play, just use the command "PLAY" and the name of the flic file that you want to display:

```
play some.fli
```

Play will display that flic, in a loop, at the speed value that's stored inside the flic's header. When you're done watching, hit (ESC) to exit.

Changing Speed

If the flic is moving too slow or too fast, you can alter the speed during play-back by pressing the number keys on your keyboard, from 1 to 9. Number 1 causes Play to display the flic as fast as it's able. If you press 9, Play will display it very slowly.

You can also affect the playback speed by using the -s command-line switch with a number from 0 to 255, like this:

```
play some.fli -s20
```

Looping

By default, Play will keep on displaying your flic forever, or at least until you press (ESC). You can make Play run the flic a specified number of times with the -l (loop) command-line switch:

```
play some.fli -l5
```

This causes Play to display the flic five times, and then exit to a DOS command line.

Memory

Play likes to load entire flics into memory before displaying them. If it can't load the whole thing into memory, playback will be much slower. If your flics are too large for conventional memory, make sure you have plenty of expanded memory (EMS) available, using a driver like EMM386.SYS or QEMM386.SYS. Play does not support extended memory (XMS). If you can, use a driver that provides both XMS and EMS on demand. QEMM-386, 386(MAX), and the DOS 6 version of EMM386.SYS all support this feature. See the documentation for your memory manager for more information on setting it up.

Changing Luminence

You can adjust the brightness of colors in your flic by pressing (PGUP) and (PGDN). The (PGUP) key brightens things up, and (PGDN) makes the flic darker.

SUMMARY

Now that you're filled to the brim with information about switches, widgets, and doodads that hide inside of DMorf, DTA, FLISPEED, and Play, it's a good time to just play with the programs for a while. Try some weird experiments. The next chapter has some fun with real-life examples. Perhaps you can use these for inspiration or building blocks.

For more information, read the documentation included with the programs. Each program comes with additional documentation files, which you'll find in the \MORPHING\TOOLS directory that you installed from this book's companion disks. In a few cases, you'll find details there that you won't find anywhere in this book.

Remember, all of the programs in this book are shareware, except for FLISPEED, which is free. The shareware marketing concept makes it possible for you to "kick the wheels" and take a piece of software for a drive around the block before spending any money on it. But shareware won't work without the support of its users. Support shareware.

Onward!

5

Morphing
Portfolio

CHAPTER 5

Morphing Portfolio

This chapter presents a collection of completed morph animations, which demonstrate the tools and tricks that you've already been introduced to earlier in this book. You know how to use these tricks, but these examples should give you some hints of what you can do with them. These examples showcase the different types and variations on morphing that you can achieve using the tools provided with this book. Some examples are simple, and some are weird and challenging. You'll find morphs that transform people, animals, people *and* animals, cars, robots, buildings, and more. I hope they inspire you to make your own mind-boggling morphs.

In each section of this chapter, you'll find:

◆ Sample animation frames

◆ Directions for re-creating the morph for your viewing pleasure.

◆ A description of any special DMorf or DTA tricks used

◆ Details on how the images were created or captured

In the directory, \MORPHING\CHAP5, which was created on your hard disk when you installed the companion floppy disk, there's a subdirectory for each morph. This subdirectory contains all of the images and meshes used to build the morph, along with a DOS batch file that you can use to generate the sequence.

DANNY AND GEORGE

The most amazing transformation that you'll ever see in real life is a child growing up. But it sure does take a long time! If, after a few years of waiting, you get impatient, you can speed things up with a morph. You can get a good idea of how a little boy might look as he grows up by morphing his picture into that of his father. This trick isn't exactly scientific, but it looks real and it's fun.

This sample, titled D&G, shows Danny Dolmat morph into his father, George. It's an example of the simplest and most common variety of morph, one between two human faces. It's so simple because both have all of the same features: head, hairline, eyes, ears, nose, mouth, chin, and shoulders. Only the placement is different. Figure 5-1 shows a series of frames from the morph animation.

Building the Danny and George Morph

To assemble the animation, run D&G.BAT by typing

```
cd\morphing\chap5\d&g
d&g
```

The D&G.BAT batch file, shown in Listing 5-1, will run both DMorf and DTA to create a flic called D&G.FLI.

The first command tells DMorf to load the D&G.MSH mesh file. The /GO option at the end tells it to perform the morph immediately and then exit to DOS, so once you start the batch file you won't have to click any buttons or press any keys while your machine generates the animation frames. DMorf

Figure 5-1 Danny and George morph sequence

will generate a series of Targa-format files named DG000001.TGA, DG000002.TGA, and so on.

The second command tells DTA to build the flic from all of the still pictures. The first three parameters tell DTA the name of the before picture (DANNY.TGA), the names of all the morphed in-between frames, and the after picture (GEORGE.TGA). You don't have to supply the .TGA extension because DTA assumes that is the extension for any filename that doesn't include them. The fourth parameter, /OD&G, tells DTA to name the output file "D&G". There's no need to include the .FLI extension with the filename, because DTA will figure that out on its own. The last parameter, /P, tells DTA to "Ping-Pong" the pictures in the second layer, or to add them to the flic twice, the second time in reverse order, so that the flic loops properly.

Listing 5-1 D&G.BAT

```
dmorf d&g.msh /go
dta danny dg*.tga george /od&g /p
```

Display your newly created flic by running the Play program. From the MORPHING\CHAP5\D&G subdirectory, type:

```
play d&g.fli
```

Discussion

Both pictures were scanned from family photographs using a Hewlett-Packard Scanjet IIc color flatbed scanner. The backgrounds were edited out and replaced with a neutral color using a paint program. Figure 5-2 shows the mesh used to create this morph.

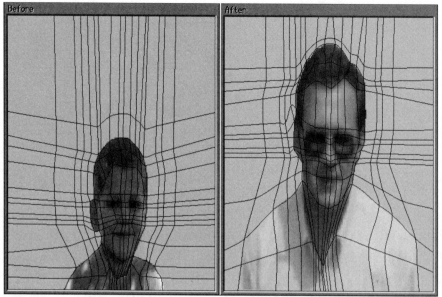

Figure 5-2 The DMorf screen

PENDRAGON AND P.J.

A common type of morph that many beginners like to try is a transformation between a husband and wife or boyfriend and girlfriend. In this sample, Pendragon Enzmann turns into his lovely wife P.J. Figure 5-3 shows a sequence of still frames from the morph.

Figure 5-3 Pendragon and P.J. morph sequence

Building the Pendragon and P.J. Morph

Change to the correct directory on your hard disk and run the PENPJ.BAT batch file:

```
cd\morphing\chap5\penpj
penpj
```

The batch file, shown in Listing 5-2, first runs DMorf against each of the three mesh files, and then generates a flic called PENPJ.FLI. Much like most of the other examples in this chapter, DMorf generates in-between frames using the PENPJ.MSH mesh file, and DTA overlays the new images (which contain transparency information in an alpha channel) over a new background image.

Listing 5-2 PEN&PJ.BAT

```
dmorf pen&pj.msh /go
dta bricks.gif /l pen.tga ppj*.tga pj.tga /p /open&pj
```

Discussion

All of the images in this morph were captured from video with a PC-Hurricane board. The pictures of Pendragon and P.J. were recorded at their place in Newton, Massachusetts. The backgrounds were removed from resulting images using Photoshop. The brick wall is from the side of a convenience store in Boston. This image was rescaled and translated to a 256-color GIF file using DTA.

Figure 5-4 shows the morphing control mesh and the pictures used to build the animation. The difficulty with this kind of a morph is: what do you do

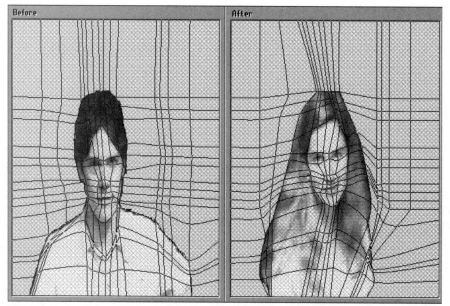

Figure 5-4 Control mesh for the Pendragon and P.J. morph

with all of the extra hair? In this morph, P.J.'s long hair is mapped to the edges of Pendragon's face and shoulders. The rest of their features are handled in a straightforward manner.

OWL/BEAR

In *Willow,* the first motion picture to use a true computer-generated morphing effect, the miniature magician Willow attempted to transform the enchanted

Figure 5-5 Owl/Bear morph sequence

sorceress Raziel from the shape of a fuzzy little squirrel-looking animal back into her original human form. Because he was a beginner at the sorcery game and kept getting the magic words wrong, he first changed her into several other animal shapes, including that of a raven, a goat, an ostrich, and a tiger, before he finally got it right. Let's try for a similar effect.

It's more difficult to morph animals than it it is to morph people, because their features don't match as well. A chihuahua and a pit bull, dogs of different breeds but still of the same species, look wildly different. Morphing between species can be even more troublesome. In this sample, titled OWLBEAR, we'll try morphing a bear into an owl. Figure 5-5 shows a series of frames from the animation.

Building the Owl/Bear Morph

From the MORPHING\CHAP5\OWLBEAR subdirectory, you can run the OWLBEAR.BAT batch file to assemble this sample morph. Type:

```
cd\morphing\chap5\owlbear
owlbear
```

The OWLBEAR.BAT batch file, shown in Listing 5-3, will run both DMorf and DTA. This DMorf command is identical to the comand used in the last example except for the new mesh-file name. It will morph the pictures BEAR.TGA and OWL.TGA to create a series of new Targa image files called OWBR0001.TGA, OWBR0002.TGA, and so on. DTA will then generate a flic file from all of those pictures called OWLBEAR.FLI. Notice the /REP9 parameters following the names of the before and after images. They instruct DTA to repeat each of those pictures 9 times, so it's displayed a total of 10 times, to make the flic pause at those points when you play it. The /REP switch won't pause properly unless a flic has a speed setting greater than 0, so

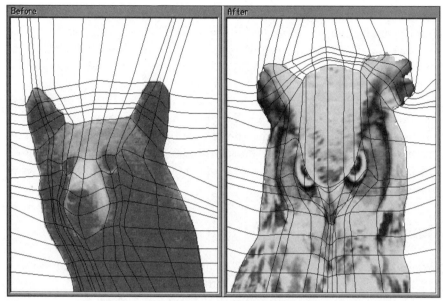

Figure 5-6 Control mesh for the Owl/Bear morph

the command also includes the parameter /S7, which sets the play rate to 7/70 (or 1/10) of a second. A player will keep each frame on the screen for that long, so the start and end frames will each be displayed for a full second.

Listing 5-3 OWLBEAR.BAT

```
dmorf owlbear.msh /go
dta bear /rep9 owbr* owl /rep9 /oowlbear /s7
```

Figure 5-7 Danny and Sarah morph sequence

Display your newly created flic by running the Play program. From the MORPHING\CHAP5\OWLBEAR subdirectory, type:

```
play owlbear.fli
```

Discussion

Both pictures were recorded on video at the Boston Museum of Science and captured with a PC-Hurricane video digitizer board (see Chapter 3, for more information on this device). The bear is stuffed, but the owl is alive.

Even though we're turning a big furry mammal into a bird, this morph turns out to be fairly simple. The bear's ears map very easily to the owl's feathery "horns." The only slight complications are turning the bear's large muzzle into a little beak, and making the bear's flat brow descend to match the owl's. Figure 5-6 shows the mesh used to create this morph.

DANNY AND SARAH

Simple morphs that transform between two people's faces are fun at first, but eventually the novelty wears off. To keep the kids interested, you'll need to find some variations on the basic effect. This sample, titled D&S, illustrates one such variation, the symmetric morph technique described in Chapter 3. In it, Danny Dolmat and his little sister Sarah stand facing each other in front of a cloudy sky. Danny begins shrinking and Sarah starts growing, until brother turns into sister and vice versa. Figure 5-7 shows a series of frames from the morph animation.

Building the Danny and Sarah Morph

Change to the D&S subdirectory and run the D&S.BAT batch file to assemble this sample morph by typing:

```
cd \morphing\chap5\d&s
d&s
```

The D&S.BAT batch file, shown in Listing 5-4, will run both DMorf and DTA. The DMorf command used in this batch file works just like those in the previous samples. It morphs the image files DSL.TGA and DSR.TGA, and creates a series of Targa files called DNSR0001.TGA, DNSR0002.TGA, and so on, up to DNSR0010.TGA.

The DTA command contains some new parameters, and also some familiar ones. The first parameter tells DTA the name of a background image, CLOUDY.TGA. The second, /L, instructs DTA to place the rest of the pictures in a second layer, in front of the background image. The next three parameters specify the names of the before picture, the morphed in-between frames, and the after picture. These files serve as the foreground pictures. Because they con-

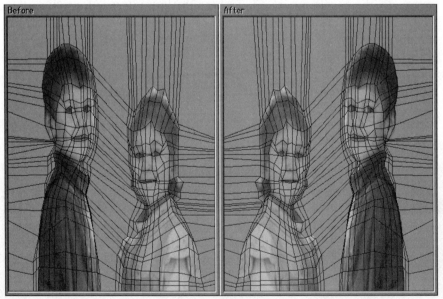

Figure 5-8 Mesh for the Danny and Sarah morph

tain transparency information in an alpha channel (as described in the section titled "The Background Problem" in Chapter 3), the background image shows through in some places.

The next-to-last parameter, /P, tells DTA to "Ping-Pong" the pictures in the second layer. If you wanted to Ping-Pong pictures in the first layer, then you'd need another /P parameter before the /L switch. There's no need to, however, because in this example the first layer contains only one picture, which will be repeated for all ten frames in the animation. The final parameter, /OD&S, tells DTA what to call the flic that it creates.

Listing 5-4 D&S.BAT

```
dmorf d&s.msh /go
dta cloudy.tga /l dsl.tga dnsr*.tga dsr.tga /p /od&s
```

Display your newly created flic by running the Play program. From the MORPHING\CHAP5\D&S subdirectory, type:

```
play d&s.fli
```

Discussion

The first picture, DSL.TGA, was scanned with an HP Scanjet color scanner and DeskScan for Windows software. The background was removed using DMorf's editing feature (described in Chapter 3). The second picture, DSR.TGA, is just a horizontally flipped version of the same picture.

Like the pictures, the control mesh is symmetrical: the left half of the mesh is a mirror image of the right half. Figure 5-8 shows the mesh used to create this morph. See Chapter 3 for a discussion of symmetric morphs.

EROSION

Erosion is another natural transformation that you can see in real life if you wait long enough. Rocks, statues, and other objects that are continuously exposed to the elements tend to wear away over the years of being bombarded by natural forces like wind and water. Let's speed things up again by morphing some images.

In this example morph, titled Erosion, a shiny red ball rests on a reflective plane. The ball's surface grows dull and rough. The pits in the surface deepen

Figure 5-9 Final morph sequence for the Erosion morph

and enlarge until you can see through holes in the shell. Figure 5-9 shows a sequence of frames from the Erosion animation.

Building the Erosion Morph

Change to the correct directory on your hard disk and run the ERODE.BAT batch file. Type:

```
cd\morphing\chap5\erode
erode
```

The ERODE.BAT batch file, shown in Listing 5-5, first runs the ERODE.MSH mesh file through DMorf, creating a series of Targa files. Next it runs DTA, which generates a flic called ERODE.FLI by overlaying the resulting TGA files on top of a background image.

Listing 5-5 ERODE.BAT

```
dmorf erode.msh /go
dta sky.gif /l regular.tga fade*.tga eroded.tga  /p /oerode
```

Discussion

You can create very realistic and amazing pictures and animations from just a description using a 3-D rendering program like Polyray or POV-Ray. Texture-mapping techniques allow you to apply all kinds of finishes to objects, from checkered and striped patterns to marble and wood. You can even do a nice pitted metal surface. It's more difficult to transform one texture to another one. It *can* be done, but you can do it faster and easier by morphing the images.

Both pictures were rendered using Polyray. The data files for the pictures are available on the companion disk. The first picture, REGULAR.TGA, is from REGULAR.PI, and the other, ERODED.TGA is from ERODED.PI.

Figure 5-10 shows the DMorf before and after windows for the Erosion morph. You'll notice that no mesh is visible. None is required, because the geometry of the two scenes is identical. Only the texture changes, so a simple fade is the only effect required.

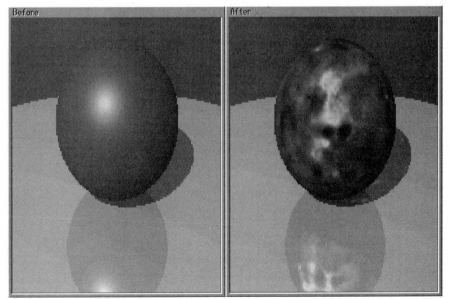

Figure 5-10 Mesh for the Erosion morph

DOG

It's always fun to morph a human being into an animal, and werewolf transformations are especially amusing. Almost everybody's seen werewolf transformations: in the old Lon Chaney *Wolf Man* movies, in more recent horror films like *The Howling* or *An American Werewolf in London,* or in Michael Jackson's "Thriller" music video. But most of those were done with traditional special effects, such as a series of simple fades between different made-up faces, or air bladders under makeup.

A werewolf morph usually looks more authentic than those techniques and probably would cost a lot less because you don't have to pay the makeup people to create as many intermediate designs—or the actor to sit through them. You'll still have to pay them something, because severe changes look best if you stage them as a series of morphs instead of trying to do it all at once. In the film *Indiana Jones and the Last Crusade,* for example, Industrial Light and Magic created an aging and decomposing effect by morphing between an actor and three puppets, each more disgusting than the one before it.

In this sample morph, titled Dog, the author succumbs to the full moon and finds himself transformed into his Aunt Rosie's dog, Alex. Figure 5-11 shows a sequence of frames from the Dog morph animation.

Building the DOG Morph

Change to the correct directory on your hard disk and run the DOG.BAT batch file. Type:

```
cd\morphing\chap5\dog
dog
```

Figure 5-11 Final morph sequence for Dog

The DOG.BAT batch file, shown in Listing 5-6, first runs DMorf against the DOG.MSH mesh file, and generates a flic called DOG.FLI.

Listing 5-6 DOG.BAT

```
dmorf dog.msh /go
dta stars /l moon /st0,0 /l dkm /rep5 ddog* hound /odog /rep5 /p
```

This animation uses three image layers. The first, STARS.TGA, is an empty starfield. The second, MOON.TGA, which follows the first /L (layer) parameter, is an image of a full moon. The files that make up the morphing sequence, following the second /L parameter, make up the top layer of the animation.

The moon is a separate layer instead of part of the starry sky because that makes it easy to move it around to see if it looks better in a different position. The /ST (starting location) option tells DTA to place the top-left corner of the moon image at the top-left corner of the screen. Without this option, the moon would have been placed in the center of the screen, right behind the head, because that image is smaller than the other two.

Again, we use the /REP parameter to make the animation pause at the beginning and end of the morph sequence.

Discussion

The first picture, DKM.TGA, was captured from video tape using a PC-Hurricane video digitizer (described in Chapter 3). The background was removed using DMorf's Edit screen (also explained in Chapter 3). The second, DOG.TGA, was scanned from a family photograph and manipulated into his shirt using Photoshop for Windows (he was originally wearing a T-shirt). The background image, STARS.TGA, was generated using POV-Ray. The other

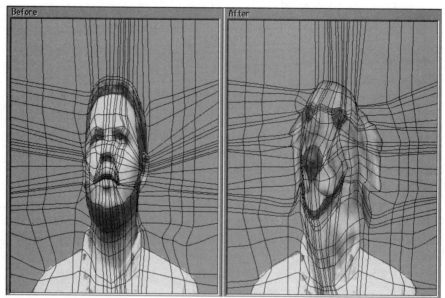

Figure 5-12 Mesh for the Dog Morph

background image, MOON.TGA, comes from a video of the giant model moon in the Boston Museum of Science. The backgrounds of DOG.TGA and MOON.TGA were cleared out and set to a unique color using Photoshop, then chroma-keyed to transparency with DMorf.

Figure 5-12 shows the mesh that was used to create the morph sequence.

CARS

In Franz Kafka's novel *The Metamorphosis,* the main character is transformed into a disgusting insect. It would be nice to duplicate that effect, if any pictures of giant bugs were readily available. We'll have to make do with another kind of bug—the automotive variety. This scene, titled Cars, opens with a picture of an ancient Volkswagen bug. As you watch, the bug transforms into a modern sports car. Probably many owners of such clunkers wish that this would happen to *their* cars, but if you have kids who are big fans of Disney's *Herbie the Love Bug* movies, you might want to try re-creating this morph in reverse. Figure 5-13 shows a sequence of frames from the car morph animation.

Figure 5-13 Final morph sequence for Cars

Building the Cars Morph

Change to the correct directory on your hard disk and run the CARS.BAT batch file:

```
cd\morphing\chap5\cars
cars
```

The batch file, shown in Listing 5-7, first runs DMorf against the mesh file, and morphs between the two automobile pictures, BUG.TGA and SPCAR.TGA. It creates a series of TGA output files, called CARS0001.TGA, CARS0002.TGA, and so on. Next, DTA compiles all of these image files into a flic animation file called CARS.FLI.

Listing 5-7 CARS.BAT

```
dmorf cars.msh /go
dta bug.tga cars*.tga spcar.tga /p /ocars.fli
```

Figure 5-14 Mesh for Cars

Discussion

Both of these pictures were taped with a camcorder and captured using a PC-Hurricane board. The first car (BUG.TGA) was parked at the side of Boston's Dartmouth Street, the second (CAR2.TGA) in the parking lot of the Route 128 Commuter Rail station. I made the backgrounds transparent using DMorf's Edit feature.

Figure 5-15 Final morph sequence for Dino-Boy

Some of the curves and angles in the two pictures caused spline difficulties, so this morph required extra control points to keep them stable, especially in the forward end of each car. Figure 5-14 shows the mesh used to create the morph animation.

DINO-BOY

Most people, especially kids, love dinosaurs. We probably wouldn't be quite so enthusiastic about them if they were up and around and eating people. Fortunately, they're all safely dead, removed from the scene by a giant aster-oid that struck the earth or by some other natural cataclysm. Or are they real-ly gone? Maybe they're still around, but in disguise. In this morph (see the sample frames in Figure 5-15), we transform a little boy into a giant Tyrannosaurus Rex.

Building the Dino-Boy Morph

To assemble the Dino-Boy animation using the prepared batch file, switch to the correct directory and run the batch file by typing:

```
cd\morphing\chap5\dino
dino
```

The DINO.BAT batch file, shown in Listing 5-8, runs both DMorf and DTA. It first runs DMorf against the mesh file, and then generates a flic called DINOBOY.FLC by overlaying the resulting TGA files on top of a background image.

The first line tells DMorf to process the morph and then continue on to the next line in the batch file. It will transform BRICK.TGA, a picture of a little boy, into REX.TGA, a picture of a giant Tyrannosaurus Rex, creating a series of Targa-format files called DINO0001.TGA, DINO0002.TGA, and so on. The second command builds a flic called DINOBOY.FLI by overlaying these pictures on top of a background image called GRASSY.TGA.

Listing 5-8 DINOBOY.BAT

```
dmorf dinoboy.msh /go
dta grassy.tga /l brick.tga dino*.tga rex.tga.tga /p /odinoboy
```

Discussion

Both of these pictures were taped with a camcorder and captured using a PC-Hurricane board. The first is a posed picture of Michael "Brick" Maloney, the seven-year-old son of some friends of mine. The second is of the central attraction of the Boston Museum of Science's dinosaur section, a humungous model of a Tyrannosaurus Rex. The background image, GRASSY.TGA, was captured the same way, but it didn't come out right. A hill in the image came out completely

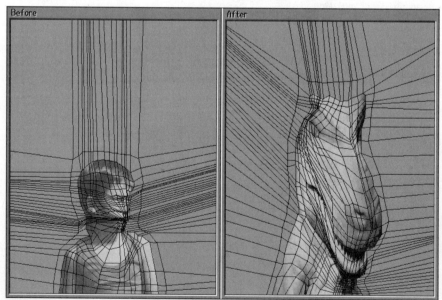

Figure 5-16 Mesh for Dino-Boy

black because of bad lighting. Photoshop came to the rescue with its noise and motion-blur filters, turning the black hill into a pleasant-looking grassy field.

Figure 5-16 shows the mesh used to create the morph animation.

The details of this mesh are extremely tight, especially on the two faces, so see the close-ups in Figures 5-17 and 5-18.

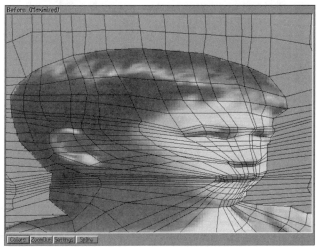

Figure 5-17 Close-up of Brick's face

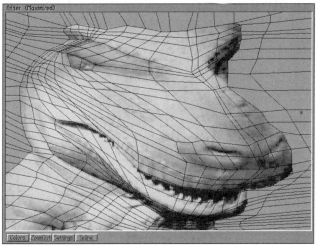

Figure 5-18 Close-up of T-Rex's face

Figure 5-19 Final morph sequence for Roofs

ROOFS

People, animals, spheres, cars, and robots aren't all that you can morph. You can do architecture, too. Roofs, a simple example of an architectural metamorphosis, morphs a regular chimney into an ornamental turret. Figure 5-19 shows a sequence of frames from the Roofs morph.

Building the Roofs Morph

Change to the correct directory on your hard disk and run the ROOFS.BAT batch file by typing:

```
cd\morphing\chap5\roofs
roofs
```

The batch file, shown in Listing 5-9, first runs DMorf against the mesh file, and then generates a flic called ROOFS.FLC.

Listing 5-9 ROOFS.BAT

```
dmorf roofs.msh /go
dta chimney.tga roof*.tga thingie.tga /p /r6
```

Discussion

Both of these pictures were taped with a camcorder at the Route 128 Amtrak/Commuter Rail train station in Westwood, Massachusetts, and captured with a PC-Hurricane board. That steeplelike structure is on top of the main station building, and the chimney comes from the little waiting room/coffee shop on the other side of the tracks.

This morph is a perfect example of when *not* to spline your control meshes. All of the edges in both pictures are straight lines, and you want them to stay that way. Figure 5-20 shows what the same morph sequence looks like if you were to run it with the Spline Meshes option turned on.

Figure 5-21 shows the mesh used to create the morph animation.

FLYING

At least as early as the days when ancient Greeks told each other tales of Daedalus, Icarus, and their wings made of wax and feathers, people have dreamed of being able to fly through the air like birds. Naturally, human flight became a very popular and inspiring special effect once movies and television

Figure 5-20 Splined version of the Roofs morph

came into existence. Special effects artists have made people fly using many different techniques, from hand-drawn animation in early Superman serials, to throwing or rocket-launching dolls through the air, to suspending an actor with wires in front of a projection of a cloudy sky. In the most convincing

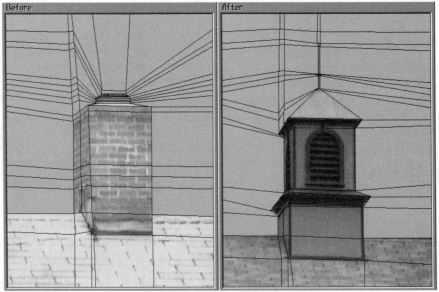

Figure 5-21 Mesh for Roofs

such effect, Christopher Reeve flew while suspended by a cable from a crane in the film *Superman: the Movie.*

Using DMorf's warping feature, you can build your own low-budget flying animation. In this sample warping sequence, titled Flying, Sarah Dolmat flies across the sky. Figure 5-22 shows a series of frames from this animation.

Building the Flying Warp

Change to the correct directory on your hard disk and run the FLYING.BAT batch file, by typing:

```
cd\morphing\chap5\flying
flying
```

The batch file, shown in Listing 5-10, first runs DMorf against each of the three mesh files, and then generates a flic called FLYING.FLI. The only new technique in this set of commands is the /CL (clipping) switch on the DTA command line. It instructs DTA to use only a portion of the pictures in the second image layer. /CL usually takes four numbers, for the left edge of the clipping window, then the top edge, and then the width and height of the window. In this case, there are only numbers for the left edge and the width, so no vertical clipping will take place. There will be more details about why we're using the clipping switch in the "Discussion."

139

Figure 5-22 Frames from the Flying warp sequence

Listing 5-10 FLYING.BAT

```
dmorf flying.msh /go
dta cloudy.gif /l sarah.tga fly*.tga /cl320,,320 /oflying
```

Discussion

As mentioned before, this is a warp, not a morph. As such, there's only one picture: SARAH.TGA. The control mesh for this sequence, shown in Figure 5-23, causes Sarah to be moved from the left edge of the window to the right edge. The picture looks squashed horizontally when displayed in DMorf

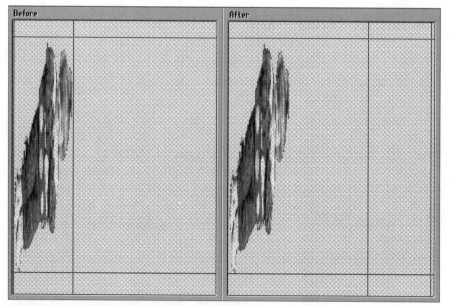

Figure 5-23 Mesh for the Flying warp

because it's very wide: the dimensions are 960 x 133 pixels. The whole picture of Sarah is located in the first one-third of the picture. The clipping window defined in the DTA command line causes only the second third of the picture to show up on the screen when the animation plays. At first, Sarah doesn't show up on the screen at all. During the course of the warping sequence, Sarah moves inside of the window, becoming visible. She travels across to the final third of the picture, where she disappears from the right edge of the clipping window.

SARAH.TGA was first scanned from a photograph using a Hewlett-Packard Scanjet II flatbed scanner. The original background was made transparent using a combination of Photoshop's path, selection, and channel facilities. Then the picture of Sarah was rotated and extended to its unusual dimensions, also in Photoshop.

WATCH

Morphs don't have to make a whole lot of sense. Sometimes you can have more fun, and make a greater impression, by morphing objects that don't have much in common. In this example, titled Watch, we'll take a pocket watch and turn it into the planet Earth. Figure 5-24 shows a sequence of still frames from the Watch animation.

Building the Watch Morph

Change to the correct directory on your hard disk and run the WATCH.BAT batch file:

```
cd\morphing\chap5\watch
watch
```

Figure 5-24 Frames from the Watch morph

The batch file, shown in Listing 5-11, first runs DMorf against each of the three mesh files, and then generates a flic called WATCH.FLI.

Listing 5-11 WATCH.BAT

```
dmorf watch.msh /go
dta stars.gif /l watch.tga wrth*.tga earth.tga /p /owatch
```

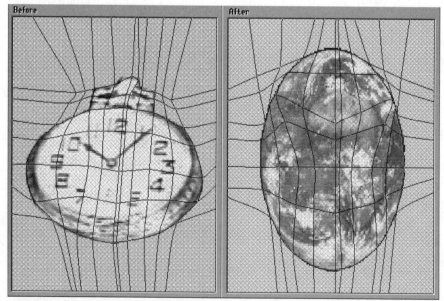

Figure 5-25 Mesh for the Watch morph

Discussion

The picture of the watch was recorded on video from the window of a jewelry store, and transferred from video to a computer image using the PC-Hurricane digitizer board. The image of the earth comes from a NASA space photograph, available on CompuServe's SPACEFORUM as SH24.GIF. The background image, STARS.GIF, was rendered with POV-Ray. It's the same image we used for the background in the Dog morph.

Figure 5-25 shows the morphing control mesh and the pictures used to build the animation. The internal details of the two shapes don't have to match exactly, because there aren't any features that naturally correspond. We'll just let them fade and concentrate on the silhouettes instead. The only tricky part is to get the knob at the end of the watch to compress down to the smooth round edge at the top of the earth.

PLANETARY EVOLUTION

In spite of what you saw in the previous morphing example, the earth didn't really develop from a giant space pocket watch. In the real universe, it was a slow process in which space dust collected into a huge cloud. Rings developed around a central clump that would eventually become the sun. The third ring from the center compressed down to a sphere of molten rock. It cooled down and grew a crust. Eventually the whole surface became solid, and cracks grew. Gases escaped in clouds from those cracks, eventually covering the entire planet. Rain came, and oceans filled the low spots. Green stuff grew on the dirt, and eventually the clouds subsided. From space, this whole many-million-year process might have looked a bit like this sample morph, titled Planet. Figure 5-26 shows a sequence of still frames from this morph animation.

Building the Planet Morph

Change to the correct directory on your hard disk and run the PLANET.BAT batch file:

```
cd\morphing\chap5\planet
planet
```

The batch file, shown in Listing 5-12, first runs DMorf against each of the seven mesh files, and then generates a flic called PLANET.FLI.

Listing 5-12 PLANET.BAT

```
dmorf shrink.msh /go
dmorf swirl.msh /go
dmorf solid.msh /go
dmorf crack.msh /go
dmorf leak.msh /go
dmorf atmo.msh /go
dmorf clear.msh /go
dta stars.gif /l @planet.lst /ch0,0,0 /dr
```

The /GO option at the end of each of the first seven commands tells DMorf to load the specified mesh file, perform the morph, and then exit. As you can see from the /L parameter in the final command, it's a multilayer animation like some of the other samples. There are so many different files involved in this animation that a DTA command listing them all is a bit unwieldy. Instead, there's a file called PLANET.LST, shown in Listing 5-13 which lists each of the files that makes up the second layer. The @planet.lst parameter tells DTA to use these filenames .

Listing 5-13 PLANET.LST

```
cloud.gif
shrn*.tga
molten.gif
swrl*.tga
crusty.gif
sold*.tga
shell.gif
crck*.tga
```

```
cracked.gif
clds*.tga
leaking.gif
atms*.tga
atmos.gif
erth*.tga
earth.gif
```

Because the images we're using are all 256-color GIF files, they don't contain any transparency information. They do all contain black backgrounds, so we can use DTA's chroma-key feature to make those backgrounds transparent. The /CH0,0,0 parameter tells DTA to make each black pixel transparent. The 0,0,0 represents black because black contains no red, no green, and no blue. This animation contains very wide variations in color—more than the 256-color flic format can handle very well—so we add the final switch, /DR, to make DTA use a random dither when it translates all of the pictures to the new 256-color palette.

Discussion

The final picture in this sequence, EARTH.GIF, is a shrunken and modified version of a NASA space photograph, found on CompuServe's SPACEFORUM as SH24.GIF. All of the others were painted from scratch and manipulated with Photoshop.

Figure 5-27 shows the morphing control mesh contained in SHRINK.MSH and the pictures, CLOUD.GIF and MOLTEN.GIF, used to build the first portion of the animation. The main effect in this portion of the animation is to make the large cloud shrink down to a planet-sized sphere, while fading from the cloud texture to a molten rock texture. In an additional trick, we make the central area of the two spheres swirl a bit.

Figure 5-28 shows the pictures and mesh for the last of the meshes, CLEAR.MSH, which morphs between ATMOS.GIF, an image of the earth covered with clouds, and EARTH.GIF. The shapes and sizes of the two versions of the planet are identical, so we could have just faded between the two pictures. The effect would be rather bland, but we can liven it up by making the patterns swirl as they fade. The circle in the middle of the planet gets rotated about ten degrees while it fades from one picture to the other.

All of the other meshes used in this morph are clones of CLEAR.MSH. They use different pictures, but the actual meshes are identical. Each different Earth sphere is exactly the same shape and size, so completely new meshes

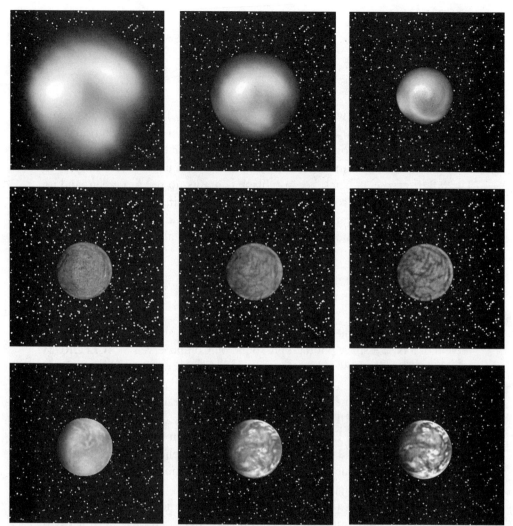

Figure 5-26 Planetary Evolution morph sequence

weren't necessary. Over the course of the whole sequence, that ten-degree rotation in each one adds up to a nice long swirling motion. The other morphs are contained in SWIRL.MSH, which morphs MOLTEN.GIF into CRUSTY.GIF (a picture of a partially crusted-over planet); SOLID.MSH, which morphs CRUSTY.GIF into SHELL.GIF (a picture of a completely solid

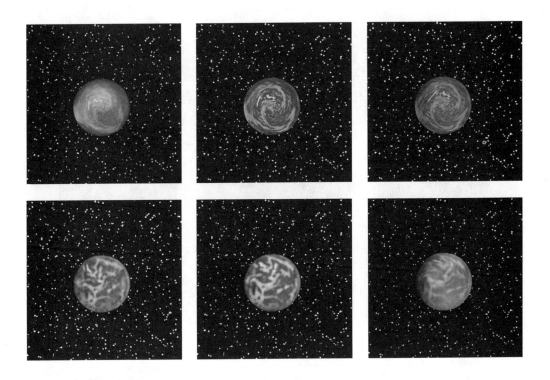

planet); CRACK.MSH, which morphs SHELL.GIF into CRACKED.GIF (which is similar to SHELL.GIF, but has a lot of cracks in the surface); LEAK.MSH, which morphs CRACKED.GIF into LEAKING.GIF (much like CRACKED.GIF, but the cracks are covered with wispy clouds); and ATMO.MSH, which morphs LEAKING.GIF into ATMOS.GIF.

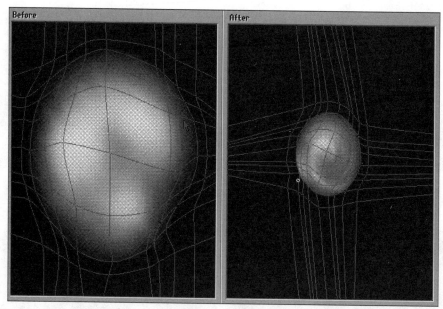

Figure 5-27 The first mesh for the Planetary Evolution morph

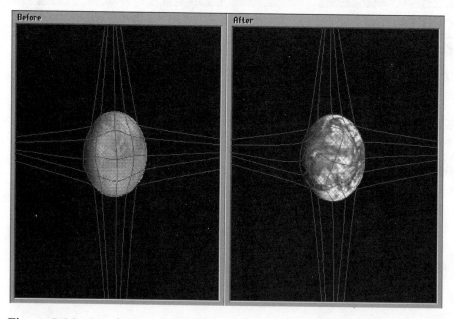

Figure 5-28 Another mesh from the Planetary Evolution morph

GENIE IN A BOTTLE

The Arabian Nights stories have inspired some great films, such as *The Thief of Baghdad,* the Sinbad movies, and Disney's recent animated *Aladdin,* and a fun television show, "I Dream of Jeanie." Much of the enjoyment derived from these movies comes from the odd and awesome creatures that populate them: genies (or djinni), rocs, and sword-fighting skeletons, and the magical objects, like flying carpets and metal songbirds. Especially popular are the genies, who when freed from lamps or bottles in which they've been imprisoned, emerge in a puff of smoke. If you free a genie, and the genie's in a good mood, he (or she) might just grant your every wish instead of chopping your head off.

In this example, smoke emerges from a golden, jewelled bottle atop a flying carpet and grows into a blue-skinned djinn. He isn't carrying a scimitar, so maybe you've got three wishes coming to you. Figure 5-29 shows some frames from the Genie animation.

Building the Genie Morph

Change to the correct directory on your hard disk and run the GENIE.BAT batch file:

```
cd\morphing\chap5\genie
genie
```

The batch file, shown in Listing 5-14, first runs DMorf against the mesh file, and then generates a flic called GENIE.FLI by overlaying the resulting TGA files on top of a background image.

The first four commands tell DMorf to create all of the in-between frames for four separate morphs. The last overlays the completed sequence on an image containing the flying carpet and genie bottle, building a flic called GENIE.FLI.

Listing 5-14 GENIE.BAT

```
dmorf fade.msh /go
dmorf smoke.msh /go
dmorf genie.msh /go
dmorf wave.msh /go
dta bottle.tga /l blank fade* puff pfsm* smoke smge* genie wave* genie2 /p /ogenie
```

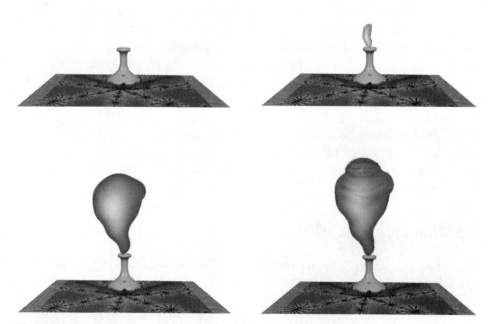

Figure 5-29 Genie in a Bottle morph sequence

Discussion

As previously mentioned, the Genie animation is composed of four separate morphs. The first, defined by the mesh file FADE.MSH, fades between a completely transparent picture called BLANK.TGA and an image of a wisp of smoke, called PUFF.TGA. Figure 5-30 shows this mesh. There aren't any mesh control points beyond those at each corner of the two pictures, because we don't need to warp any objects. PUFF.TGA was painted from scratch in Photoshop's paint and image-processing program, and the background was chroma-keyed to transparency with DMorf's editing facility. BLANK.TGA is a copy of PUFF.TGA with the smoke painted out in DMorf.

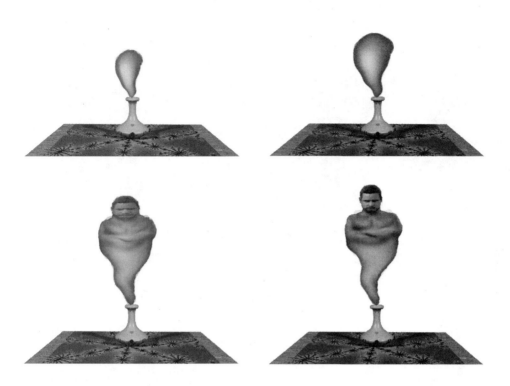

The second portion, defined in SMOKE.MSH, morphs between PUFF.TGA and an image of a much larger puff of smoke, called SMOKE.TGA. Figure 5-31 shows the mesh used to create the morph. It's a very simple mesh, because all we have to do is map the edges of the two smoke puffs. The interior areas contain no features. SMOKE.TGA was also painted in Photoshop.

The third morph, defined in GENIE.MSH, transforms the large puff of smoke into the body of a genie, floating above the bottle. Figure 5-32 shows the mesh used to create this portion of the animation. This one's a bit more complicated, because the genie's features need be mapped to evenly-spaced points in the smoke-puff. The genie picture, GENIE.TGA, started its life as a video capture of the author, but it was massively fiddled with in Photoshop.

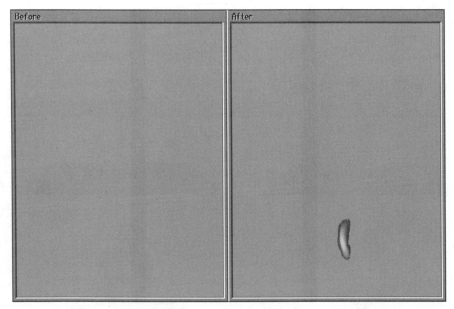

Figure 5-30 First mesh for the Genie morph

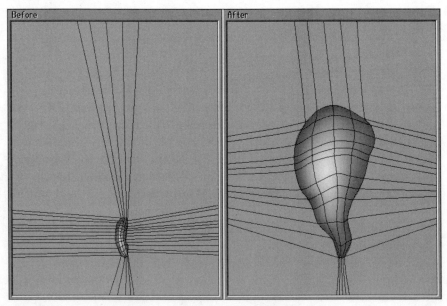

Figure 5-31 Second mesh for the Genie morph

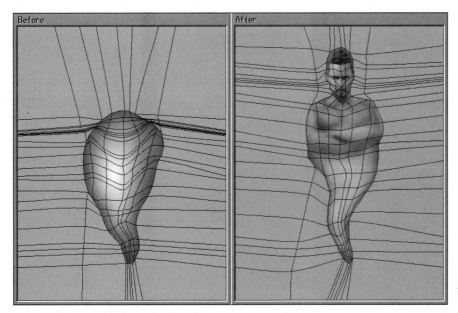

Figure 5-32 Third mesh for the Genie morph

The final section, defined in WAVE.MSH, is actually a warp, not a morph. It causes the genie's smoky lower portion to twist around as if in the wind. Figure 5-33 shows the mesh used to create this portion.

BOTTLE.TGA, the background picture containing a genie bottle and flying carpet, was built using Alexander Enzmann's shareware rendering program Polyray. The Stone Soup Group's FRACTINT provided a fractal pattern for the carpet, and the fringe at the ends of the carpet is a product of Photoshop's noise and motion-blur filters. The copy of BOTTLE.TGA on the disk is a rather low-resolution image because of disk-space restraints, but if you have Polyray and would like to rebuild it at higher resolution, you'll find the required data files in the directory for this morph. BOTTLE.PI is the Polyray input file, RUG.TGA is the fractal pattern for the flying carpet, and FRINGE.TGA is the pattern for the carpet's gold fringe.

ROBOT

In one of the more fascinating special effects sequences in the film *Terminator 2: Judgment Day*, the evil terminator transforms from a mess of liquid metal goop

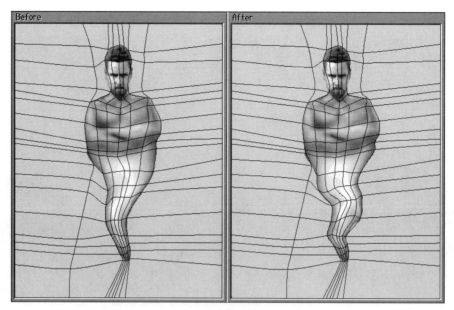

Figure 5-33 Fourth mesh for the Genie morph

into a human-shaped metal body and then into a human being. The special effects wizards used a combination of 3-D and 2-D morphing techniques to create this effect, but we can do a reasonable facsimile using just 2-D morphing. In this sample morph, a shiny metallic sphere starts pulsating and flowing. The shape flattens and stretches, and a bulbous nodule grows on top. The main body of the sphere forms into robotic shoulders and arms, while the wart on top develops into a robot head. Finally, the robot tranforms into a human being. Figure 5-34 shows a sequence of still frames from the Robot animation.

Building the Robot Morph

Change to the correct directory on your hard disk and run the ROBOT.BAT batch file:

```
cd\morphing\chap5\robot
robot
```

The batch file, shown in Listing 5-15, first runs DMorf against each of the three mesh files, and then generates a flic called ROBOT.FLI.

Listing 5-15 ROBOT.BAT

```
dmorf sphblb.msh /go
dmorf blobs.msh /go
dmorf blbrob.msh /go
dmorf robdav.msh /go
dta cloudy /l sphere spbl* blob1 blbs* blob2 blro* robot roda* dkm /p /orobot /r6
```

The /GO option at the end of each of the first four commands tells DMorf to load the specified mesh file, perform the morph, and then exit. Once you start the batch file you won't have to click any buttons or press any keys while your machine generates the animation frames for all four sequences.

The final command's a bit more complicated. Most of the parameters (the ones that don't begin with a "/") are filenames. For example, "cloudy" is a background image of a cloudy sky. Because there's no extension supplied with the filename, DTA assumes that it's a Targa-format file called CLOUDY.TGA. The ones that do end with "/" are switches, which tell DTA what to do. The /L option tells DTA to separate the background picture into one image layer, and all of the other pictures into a second layer that will be superimposed on the first layer. The /P option causes the pictures in the second layer to "Ping-Pong," or repeat in reverse order at the end of the animation. It only affects that layer because it appears after the /L. The /OROBOT option tells DTA to name the resulting flic ROBOT. The /R6 option tells DTA to create a 640 x 480-pixel resolution FLC file instead of the default 320 x 200-pixel FLI file.

Discussion

The Robot morph is actually four separate morphs created with five separate still pictures. (Each row of five frames in Figure 5-34 represents a single morph.) The first sequence is a transition between a perfect sphere (SPHERE.TGA) and a not-quite spherical blobby shape (BLOB1.TGA). The second sequence morphs between BLOB1.TGA and another blob (BLOB2.TGA), which is shaped a bit more like the head and shoulders of a person. The third portion morphs between that second blob and the robot's head and shoulders (ROBOT.TGA). The final piece morphs between the robot's head and shoulders and those of the author (DKM.TGA).

The first four pictures used in this morph were created using Alexander Enzmann's Polyray rendering program. Polyray can automatically make the background of the pictures transparent, so no editing or additional processing was necessary. If you have Polyray and would like to experiment with the

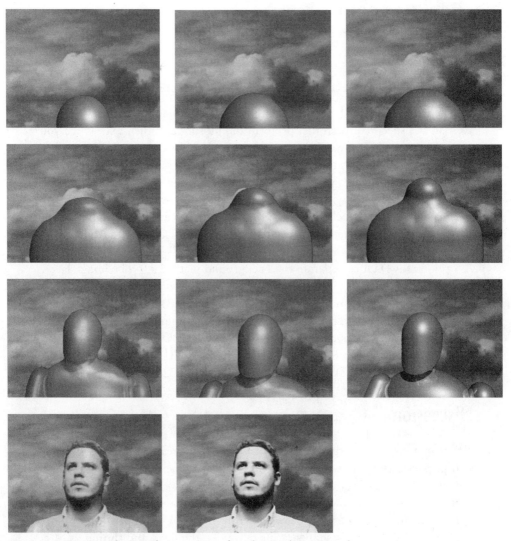

Figure 5-34 Final morph sequence for the Robot morph

data files, they are on this book's companion disk. They are SPHERE.PI, BLOB1.PI, BLOB2.PI, and ROBOT.PI. For more information about Polyray, see *Making Movies on the PC*, by David Mason and Alexander Enzmann and *Animation How-To CD*, by Jeff Bowermaster (both published by Waite Group Press). The final picture was captured from videotape using a PC-Hurricane video digitizer (described in Chapter 3) and edited using DMorf's Edit screen (also explained in Chapter 3).

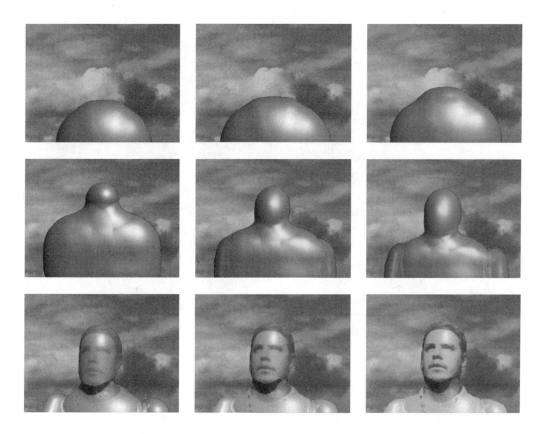

Figure 5-35 shows the morphing control mesh and the pictures used to build the first quarter of the animation. This one is pretty simple because the silhouettes of the two objects are similar in shape if not size. The main effect of this stage is to flatten the sphere on top. A second effect, obvious only in the object's shading, is to make it thinner in the front-to-back direction.

Figure 5-36 shows the pictures and mesh that were used in the middle third of the morph. In this morph, we transform one blobby-looking shape into

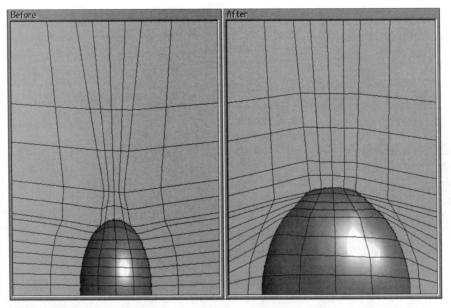

Figure 5-35 First mesh for the Robot morph

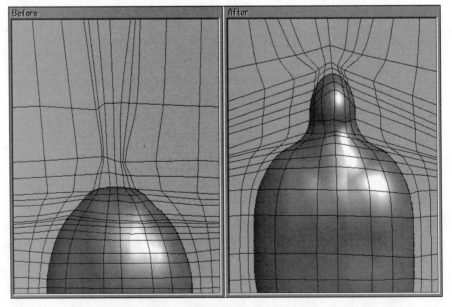

Figure 5-36 Second mesh for the Robot morph

another blobby-looking shape. The trouble spot here is making the flat area on the first blob grow into the knobby protrusion on the second blob.

Figure 5-37 shows the third mesh and set of pictures used to create this animation. Like the first, this one isn't so tough because the object's shapes are very similar. The toughest part is getting the shoulders to look right, because the robot has separate arms and the blob doesn't.

Figure 5-38 shows the pictures and mesh for the final portion of the morph. In addition to shoulder-matching problems much like the previous part, there's a problem getting the faces matched right because one has human features on it and the other doesn't. The trick to getting this right is to copy the layout of control points on the face in the second picture over to the first.

SUMMARY

This chapter demonstrated many ways to use DMorf and DTA to create an assortment of special effects. We've transformed people, animals, cars, buildings, and even a robot. Some of the examples linked multiple morphs together

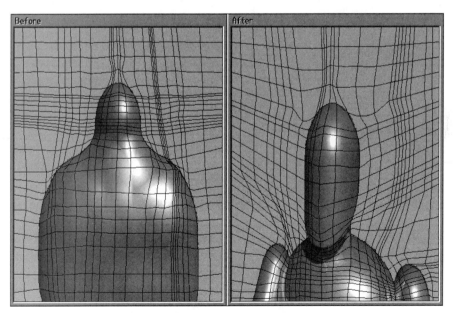

Figure 5-37 Third mesh for the Robot morph

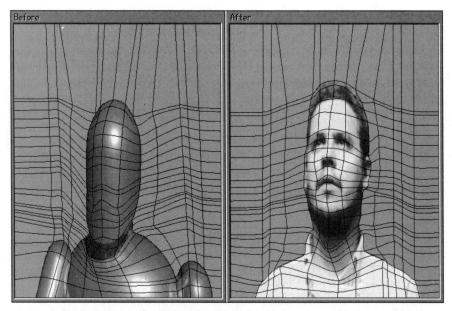

Figure 5-38 Fourth mesh for the Robot morph

to create effects that would have been impossible—or at least unconvincing—with single-step morphs. Some superimposed pictures on other pictures. I hope you've gotten some new ideas, and had some fun at the same time.

THE FAT LADY SINGS

You've learned how to capture and create your own pictures, how to create control meshes, how to edit pictures so that their backgrounds are transparent, and how to composite multiple image layers. You've studied all of the hidden switches and dials in the DMorf and DTA programs, and how to use FLISPEED and Play. This book has come to a close, but you're still just beginning. Now it's time to apply what you've learned by creating your own morphing animations. The possibilities of morphing are limited only by your imagination and patience. Apply what you've learned and invent your own new tricks.

Morphing Magic Contest

Make a change for the better. Here's your chance to show off your digital special effects, and dazzle us by using the programs in this book to create your own morph. You don't need a studio-sized budget, just your creativity, a spectacular viewpoint, and a little spirit of competition. We're looking for innovative, dramatic, state-of-the-art morphs that show off the magic of the PC and simple animation software. Please keep the size of the morph under 1.44 MB so it fits on one 3.5" high density disk. You could quickly be on the road to riches and fame.

To enter, mail your *original morph* and source code, with the entry card on the back of this page or a 3x5 postcard that includes your name, address, daytime phone number, the title of your entry, and a brief description of the morph.

Here's what you can win:

◈ First place winner receives $1000

◈ Second place winner receives $500

◈ Third place winner receices the entire Waite Group Press library

◈ Fourth through tenth place winners receive Waite Group Press t-shirts

Rules and Regulations

Eligibility: Your submission must be submitted between December 31, 1993 and May 31, 1994; it must be created with the DTA and Dmorf programs provided in this book; and the size of the morph must be under 1.44 MB to fit on a single *high density* disk.

Dates and deadlines: Entries must be received at the address provided by 5PM, May 31, 1994. Winners will be notified by August 31, 1994.

Preparation of entries: Only one morph may be submitted per entry, but you may enter as often as you like. Entries must be on a 3.5-inch disk and each disk must be labeled with your name, phone number, and the name of the flic. Waite Group Press is not responsible for lost or damaged entries. Waite Group Press will not return any entries unless entrants include a self-addressed stamped envelope designated for that purpose with their entry.

Judging and prizes: Morphs will be judged on the basis of technique, creativity, and presentation by a panel of judges from Waite Group Press. Winners will be notified by August 31, 1994. For the names of the "Morphing Magic Contest" winners and their entries, send a self-addressed, stamped envelope, after September 15, 1994, to: Waite Group Press "Morphing Magic Contest" Winner, 200 Tamal Plaza, Corte Madera, CA 94925.

Etc: No purchase necessary. Waite Group Press "Morphing Magic Contest" is subject to all federal, state, local, and provincial laws and regulations and is void where prohibited. Waite Group Press "Morphing Magic Contest" is not open to employees of The Waite Group, Inc., Publishers Group West, participating promotional agencies, any WGP distributors, and the families of any of the above. By entering the "Morphing Magic Contest," each contestant warrants that he or she is the original author of the work submitted, non-exclusively licenses The Waite Group, Inc. to duplicate, modify, and distribute the flic, and agrees to be bound by the above rules.

Name_____ Daytime Phone_____

Address _____

City _____ State _____ Zip _____

Entry (file name) _____

What should we know about this morph?_____

_____

_____

_____

Send entries to: "Morphing Magic Contest"

                      Waite Group Press

                      200 Tamal Plaza

                      Corte Madera, CA 94925

I signify that the enclosed is my own original work and that I abide by all rules described in "Morphing Magic Contest"

Signature _____

INDEX

24-bit color, 48
24-bit images, 65
32-bit TGA setting, 56
2-D interpolative splines, 27
2-D morphing, 6, 10-11
3-D morphing, 5-6, 10-11

A

AADEMO, 96
AAPLAY, 96
Abyss, The, 10
after picture
    creating mesh for, 64
After window, 87
AFTER.TGA, 92
alpha byte, 48
alpha channel, 48, 54, 56, 125
alpha masks, 49
Alpha panel, 49, 55, 85-86
Altered States, 9
America OnLine, 44
American Werewolf in London, 9, 12, 128
ANI file format, 15, 94
animals
    morphing, 120-123

Animate Plus, 94
animation. *see also* DTA
    changing speed, 36
    creating with DMorf, 60
    example portfolio, 115-160
    moving objects, 60
    multilayer, 144
    overview, 15
Animation How-To CD, 43, 156
Animator, 15, 96, 98
Animator Pro, 91
approximation, 27
Arabian Nights, 149
ARJ file format, 94
ARJ.EXE, 94
art
    computer-generated, 44
artifacts
    removing from morphs, 31-34
ASCII text file, 88
ATMOS.GIF, 145, 147
Auberjonois, Rene, 11
AUTOEXEC.BAT, xv, 72
AVI file format, 15

B

Babylon 5 television program, 11
backgrounds, 47-57
BEAR.TGA, 121
Beauty's Beast, 8
Before window, 86
BEFORE.TGA, 92
BIKE.TGA, 54-55
BIX (Byte Information Exchange), 44
Black or White video, 12
BLANK.TGA, 150
BLOB1.PI, 156
BLOB2.PI, 156
BLOB1.TGA, 155
BLOB2.TGA, 155
blue screen. *see* chroma-keying
blurring, 105
BMP/DIB file format, 94
BMP file format, 42
BOTTLE.PI, 153
BOTTLE.TGA, 153
Bowermaster, Jeff, 43, 156
Braque, 13
BRICK.TGA, 134
Brigman, Bud and Lindsay, 10
buffers
    DMorf, 72
BUG.TGA, 131-132
buildings
    morphing, 136-137
bulletin board services (BBSs), 44
Byrne, David, 12

C

cache, 72
camcorders, 20, 40, 54, 132, 134, 137
capture program, 41-42
caricatures, 57-59
CARS.BAT, 131
CARS.FLI, 131
CARS2.TGA, 132
Catmull-Rom splines, 27
10cc rock band, 11
CD-ROMs, 44-45
Chaney, Lon, 8, 128

chroma-keying, 53-55, 130
Chunky mode, 83
Claymation, 57
CLEAR.MSH, 145
Clinton, Bill, 58
clip art, 20
clipping, 141
CLOUD.GIF, 145
CLOUDS.TGA, 56
CLOUDY.TGA, 124, 155
Coffee, tea, or SEGA?! commercial, 13
COL file format, 98
Color dialog box, 55
color-reduction methods, 98
colors
    changing lunimence, 111
    chroma-keying concerns, 53-54
    controlling, 85-86
    in DMorf processing, 22
    RGB, 48
    selecting, 98-99
Colors dialog box, 49, 55
command-line switches
    DMorf, 71-73
    DTA, 91-109
    FLISPEED, 109-110
    Trilobyte Play, 111
commands. *see* under DMorf, DTA, FLISPEED,
    Trilobyte Play
Commodore Amiga computers, 11
communication software, 44
COMPED.TGA, 56
compositing, 48, 56
compressed files, 87-88
compression programs, xvi
CompuServe, 43-44, 143
computer-generated art, 44
Computer Shopper, 40
CONFIG.SYS, 72
contest
    Morphing Magic, 161-162
control mesh
    for animation, 60
    changing colors, 85
    copying, 58
    creating, 22-29

creating mirror, 62-64
described, 19
file format, 88-90
loading, 71
moving objects, 60
refining, 31-34
selecting pictures to morph, 20
splines, 133
symmetric, 62-63
testing, 29-31
warping effects, 57-60
control points
changing default settings for, 89-90
creating additional, 33
moving, 24
controls and screen layout
DMorf, 73-75
copyright concerns, 43
Coy, Stephen, 43
Coyote, 8
CPU
requirements, xiv
CRACKED.GIF, 147
CRACK.MSH, 147
Creme, Lyle, 11
cross-fade, 83
CRUSTY.GIF, 146
Cry video, 11
cubism, 13

D

3D-Studio, 43, 48
3D Workshop, 15, 43, 94
DANNY.TGA, 22, 29, 117
Dave's TGA Animator. *see* DTA
DeskScan for Windows, 125
D&G.BAT, 116
D&G.FLI, 116
D&G.MSH, 116
DG.MSH, 29
DG2.MSH, 33
dialog boxes
changing default values in, 88-89
Pictures, 86-88
Screen Colors, 85-86

Settings, 82-85
DINO.BAT, 133-134
DINOBOY.FLC, 133
DINOBOY.FLI, 134
dinosaur morph, 133-135
disk compression programs, xvi
disk space requirements, xiv
dissolves, 8, 12
dithering, 99-102
djinni morph, 149
DKM.TGA, 129, 155
DMorf
alpha-editing facility, 49
chroma-keying, 53-55
command-line syntax, 71-73
commands and settings
/1024, 72
32-bit:, 87
/GO, 73
/NOSVGA, 72
/PRELOAD, 72
A-Blur:, 82
About:, 76
After:, 87
Background:, 87
Before:, 86
Blu:, 85
Bottom-Up:, 87
Colors:, 76, 79-80
Del:, 78
Disp:, 85-86
Done:, 86
Edit:, 77
Extend:, 82
Fade 1/2:, 84-85
File:, 85
First frame/Last frame:, 84
FlipHz:, 47, 63, 77, 82
Frames:, 29, 35, 45, 58, 84
Go:, 29, 76
Grn:, 85
Hide:, 77
Just Warp:, 57-60
Just warp:, 83
Key:, 55, 82
Load:, 31, 76

DMorf Commands and Settings *continued*

Main:, 79-80
Max:, 32, 76
Other:, 32, 78, 80
Pictures:, 76
Quit:, 29, 76
Red:, 85
Reload:, 76
1→2:, 58, 60, 64, 77
2→1:, 77
RLE:, 87-88
Save:, 29, 76, 80
SaveAs:, 76, 81
Settings:, 35, 76, 80
Show in-betweens:, 84
Smooth resampling:, 46, 83
Spline:, 80
Spline always:, 83
Spline intervals:, 60, 82-83
Spline mesh:, 60, 82
Splines:, 25, 77
Swap:, 77
Tol:, 55, 82
Verbose status:, 84
Warp 1/2:, 84
ZoomIn:, 50, 78-80
ZoomOut:, 52, 79-80
copying control meshes, 58
creating
    caricatures, 57-60
    control meshes, 22-29
    mirror images, 61-64
    moving objects, 57-60
    transparent backgounds, 49-53
faster processing, 45-46
File menu panel, 75-77
generating smooth animation, 34-36
graphics modes, 72
hardware requirements, xiv
installing, xiii-xviii, 70-71
memory requirements, xv
mesh file format, 88-90
Mesh menu panel, 77-78
overview, 19
painting masks, 49-53
Pictures dialog, 86-88
quitting, 29

reference, 70-90
running under
    OS/2, xviii, 21
    Windows, xvii, 21
saving files, 29
Screen Colors dialog, 85-86
screen layout and controls, 73-75
Select option panel, 78
Settings dialog, 82-85
starting, 21-22, 31-34, 71-73
testing morphs, 29-31
tutorial, 19-36
DMORF.EXE, xiii-xiv, 70-71
DMORFNC.EXE, xiii-xiv, 70-71
DOG.BAT, 128-129
DOG.FLI, 129
DOG.MSH, 129
DOG.TGA, 129-130
DOS window
    OS/2, xviii, 21
    Windows, xvi-xvii, 21
DOSPRMFPT.PIF configuration file
    modifying, xvi-xvii
DPMI16BI.OVL, 70
DPMIINST.EXE, 70
Dracula, 8
DSL.TGA, 53, 61-62, 124-125, 56
DSR.TGA, 64, 124-125
D&S.TGA, 49
DTA
    building flics, 30-31
    chroma-keying, 55
    command-line switches, 94-109
        3/3/2 Palette (/332), 98
        3-D (/3D), 108-109
        Chroma-Key (/CH, /CT#), 106
        Creating Targa Files (/NC, /B#), 109
        External Palette (/U), 98-99
        Floyd-Steinberg (/DF), 99-102
        Frame Averaging (/A# and /T#), 105
        Frame Expansion (/X#), 108
        Grayscale Palettes (/G and /G32), 98
        Multiple Layers (/L), 105-106
        Ordered Dithering (/DO#), 100-101
        Output File Format (/F), 95
        Output File Name (/O), 95

Picture Clipping (/CL), 104
Picture Placement (/ST), 104-105
Picture Scaling (/SC), 102-103
Ping-Pong (/P), 108
Random Noise Dithering (/DR#), 102
Repeating Frames (/REP#), 97
Resolution (/R#), 95-96
Sierra-Lite (/DS), 99-102
Skipping Frames (/C#, /K#, /I#), 107-108
Speed (/S#), 96-97
command-line syntax, 91-93
compositing, 48, 56
creating
    animation files, 29-31, 92-93
faster processing, 97
gamma-correction function, 46
generating smooth animation, 35-36
installing, xiii-xviii
memory requirements, xv
modifying image brightness, 46
ping-pong effect, 56
reference, 90-109
registration, 91
resizing images, 45
running under
    OS/2, xviii
    Windows, xvii
supported file formats, 93-94
using multiple morphs, 64-65

E

EARTH.GIF, 145
EDIT, 88, 93
EMM386.EXE, xv
EMM386.SYS, 111
EMS memory. *see* expanded (EMS) memory
Enzmann, Alexander, 43, 156
ERODE.BAT, 126
ERODED.PI, 127
ERODED.TGA, 127
ERODE.FLI, 126
ERODE.MSH, 126
error-diffusion dithering methods, 99-102
error messages, 70, 90
expanded (EMS) memory, xv-xviii, 72, 111

extended (XMS) memory, xv-xviii, 72, 111
Exxon commercial, 13

F

fade effects, 127
FADE.MSH, 150
fading, 22
file downloading, 44
file formats, 22
    ARJ, 94
    AVI, 15
    BMP, 42, 94
    COL, 98
    DIB, 94
    FLI/FLC, 15, 31, 36, 94
    GIF, 22, 44, 71, 93, 145
    IMG, 22, 94
    LZH, 94
    MAP, 98
    MPEG, 15
    PCX, 94
    TGA, 22, 29, 42, 48, 56, 87-88
    ZIP, 94
files
    ATMO.MSH, 147
    installing, xiv-xv
    saving, 29
FLI/FLC file format, 15, 31, 36, 94
flic animation files, 15, 29-31, 56, 64-65, 91-93
FLISPEED
    reference, 109-110
    Speed (/S) parameter, 109-110
    when to use, 97
FLISPEED.EXE, 36
Fly, The, 8
FLYING.BAT, 139-140
FLYING.FLI, 139
foregounds, 47
Fractal Creations, 99
Fractals for Windows, 99
FRACTINT, 98-99, 153
frame rate, 15, 35
frames
    and faster processing, 45
frames-per-second (fps), 15

FRINGE.TGA, 153
Frog Prince, 8

G

Gabriel, Peter, 12
Gamma 1 panel, 85-86
Gamma 2 panel, 85-86
Genie, 44
GENIE.BAT, 149
GENIE.FLI, 149
GENIE.MSH, 151
GENIE.TGA, 151
GEORGE.TGA, 22, 29, 117
GIF file format, 22, 44, 71, 93, 145
Godley, Kevin, 11
gods
    mythological, 7-8
GRAPHDEV forum
    CompuServe, 43
Graphics Alternative BBS, 44
Graphics Forums
    CompuServe, 44
graphics modes
    DMorf, 72
    SuperVGA, xvii
GRASSY.TGA, 134
grid. *see* control mesh
Gryphon Morph, 70

H

hardware requirements, xiii-xiv
Hera, 7
Herbie the Love Bug, 130
HIMEM.SYS, xv
horizontal coordinates, 90
Howard, Ron, 9
Howling, The, 128

I

I Dream of Jeanie television series, 149
Identification section
    mesh file, 88
image buffer
    DMorf, 72
image editors, 47

Image Lab, 43, 99
image morphing. *see* 2-D morphing
images
    animating, 29-31
    clipping, 141
    compositing, 48
    copyright concerns, 43
    creating mirror, 61-64
    distorting, 58-60
    faster processing, 45
    flipping, 47
    libraries on CD-ROM, 44-45
    lighting effects, 46-47
    merging, 22
    obtaining best video frames, 42
    size in DMorf processing, 22
    sources, 20-21, 40-45, 143
    superimposing. *see* chroma-keying
    synthetic. *see* rendering
IMG file format, 22, 94
in-between meshes, 29
Indiana Jones and the Last Crusade, 10, 128
Industrial Light and Magic (ILM), 9-10, 128
Input file panel, 86-87
installation, xiii-xviii
interpolation, 27
intersection points
    moving, 24-25

J

Jackson, Michael, 12, 128
Just Warp mode, 86

K

Kafka, Franz, 130
Kirk, James T., 10

L

Landis, John, 12
laptop displays, 98
Large Marge, 10, 57
layers
    image, 56, 105-106
LEAKING.GIF, 147
LEAK.MSH, 147

legends
    shape shifting in, 7-8
Lennon, John, 11
LHA.EXE, 94
lighting, 46-47
lines
    adding to control mesh, 23-24
    curved. *see* splines
Loki, 8
Lucas, George, 9
Lugosi, Bela, 8
LZH file format, 94

M

makeup effects, 8-9
Making Movies on Your PC, 43, 156
MAP file format, 98
mapping shapes, 23-29
mask color, 52
masks
    chroma-keying, 53-55
    described, 48
    overlaying, 56
    painting, 49-53
Mason, David, 43, 156
math coprocessors, xiii-xiv, 29, 35, 70, 83
386MAX, xv, 111
maximized view, 32
Maya, 8, 11
Median-Cut, 98
MEMMAKER, xv
memory
    configuring, xv-xvii, 111
    hardware requirements, xiv
    not enough under Windows, xvi
memory-management software, xv-xvi
menus
    DMorf Edit screen, 80-82
    DMorf Main screen, 75-78
    DMorf Max screen, 78-80
Mercury, 7
Merlin, 3, 8
mesh
    control. *see* control mesh
Mesh panel, 85
metamorphosis, 3, 6-8

Metamorphosis, The, 130
Microsoft Video for Windows, 15, 94
mirror images, 61-64
misdirection, 8-9
modem, 44
MOLTEN.GIF, 145-146
monitors
    avoiding damage, 72
    VGA, 85-86, 98
MOON.TGA, 129-130
MORF
    in filenames, 87
morphing
    backgrounds, 47-56
    buildings, 136-137
    creating
        mirror images, 123-125
        video output, 65-66
    described, 3-6
    destination image, 87
    development of, 8-14
    example portfolio, 115-160
    faster processing, 45-46
    future uses, 13-14
    light in images, 46-47
    in movies and teleivision, 9-13
    with multiple morphs, 64-65
    shape shifting in myths and legends, 7-8
    source image, 86
    sources of images, 40-45
Morphing Magic Contest, 161-162
Morphing Switches menu panel, 46, 57
morphs
    Cars, 130-133
    Danny and George, 20-36, 116-118
    Danny and Sarah, 62-65, 123-125
    Dino-boy, 4-5, 133-135
    Dog, 128-130
    Erosion, 125-127
    Flying, 137-141
    Genie in Bottle, 149-153
    Owl/Bear, 120-123
    Pendragon and P.J., 118-120
    Planetary Evolution, 143-148
    Robot, 153-159
    Roofs, 136-137
    Watch, 141-143

motion blur, 105
motorcycle image, 54-55
mouse
  adding lines in control mesh, 23
  chroma-keying with, 55
  modifying lighting in images with, 47
  moving intesection points in control mesh
    with, 24
  painting masks with, 49-53
  system requirements, xiv, 22
MPEG file format, 15
MS-DOS, xv-xvi, 21, 70, 72, 88, 111
MSH file format, 29, 71, 88-90
myths
  shape shifting in, 7-8

N

Norton Utilities, 97
NTSC converters, 66
NTSC television standard, 42

O

object morphing. *see* 3-D morphing
Octree Quantization, 98
Odo, Constable, 11
online services, 44
Ono, Yoko, 11
OS/2, xviii, 21
Output files panel, 87-88
overlays, 56, 105-106
OWLBEAR.BAT, 121-122
OWLBEAR.FLI, 121
OWL.TGA, 121

P

Pacific Data Images (PDI), 9, 12
Paintbrush, 47
PAL television standard, 42
PC Animate, 91
PC-Hurricane Moviegrabber, 41-42, 54, 119,
  123, 129, 132, 134, 137, 143
PC Magazine, 40
PC Paintbrush, 94

PCX file format, 94
Pee Wee's Big Adventure, 10, 57
PENPJ.BAT, 119
PENPJ.FLI, 119
PENPJ.MSH, 119
Peterson, Mark, 99
PhotoFinish, 46-47
PhotoMorph, 70
Photoshop, 46-47, 49, 119, 130, 135, 141,
  150-151, 153
Photoshop for Windows, 129
Picasso, 13
picture buffer
  DMorf, 72
pictures. *see* images
Pictures dialog, 56, 86-88
Pictures sections
  mesh file, 89-90
Pierce, Jack, 8
ping-pong effect, 35, 56, 117, 125, 155
Pinocchio, 8
pixel colors, 48
pixels
  masking, 51-53
PKUNZIP.EXE, 94
PLANET.BAT, 144
PLANET.FLI, 144
PLANET.LST, 144-145
Playmation, 43
Polyray, 48, 91, 126, 153, 156
Popularity, 98
POV-Ray, 43, 54, 60, 91, 126, 129, 143
Presenter+, 66
Presidio 3D Workshop, 15
Prodigy, 44
ProMovie Studio, 42
Proteus, 7
PUFF.TGA, 150-151
Put a tiger in your tank commercial, 13

Q

QEMM-386, xv
QEMME86.SYS, 111
QUICKFLI, 96

R

random dithering, 145
Ray Tracing Creations, 43
RCA cable, 41, 66
Reeve, Christopher, 139
reference
    DMorf, 70-90
    DTA, 90-109
    FLISPEED, 119-110
    Trilobyte Play, 110-111
REGUALR.PI, 127
REGUALR.TGA, 127
rendered art, 44
rendering
    3-D, 126
    creating transparent backgrounds, 48-49
rendering software, 42-43, 48
REX.TGA, 134
RGB α, 48
RGB format, 55
ROBOT.BAT, 154-155
ROBOT.FLI, 154
ROBOT.TGA, 155
ROCKET.TGA, 60
ROOF.BAT, 136
ROOF.FLC, 136
RTM.EXE, 70
RUG.TGA, 153
run-length encoded (compressed) TGA files,
    87-88

S

SARAH.TGA, 140-141
Scanjet II, 40, 117, 125, 141
scanners, xiv, 20, 40, 54
Schick commercial, 13
Schwarzenegger, Arnold, 3
Screen Colors dialog, 85-86
screen layout and controls
    DMorf, 73-75
Select option box
    After option, 63
Settings dialog, 35, 82-85
Settings section

mesh file, 88-89
shadows
    modifying, 46-47
shape shifters
    in movies and television, 10-11
    in myths and legends, 7-8
SHELL.GIF, 146-147
She's Mad video, 12
SH24.GIF, 143, 145
SHRINK.MSH, 145
Sinbad movies, 149
SMOKE.MSH, 151
SMOKE.TGA, 151
Smooth mode, 83
Smythe, Douglas, 9
SOLID.MSH, 146
Somewhere in New York City album cover,
    11-12
sources
    images, 143
Space: 1999 television series, 8, 11
SPACEFORUM
    CompuServe, 143
SPCAR.TGA, 131
special effects
    computer-based, 9-13, 139-141
    traditional, 8-10, 138-139
speed setting
    changing, 36
SPEEDISK, 97
SPHERE.PI, 156
SPHERE.TGA, 155
Spline view, 25, 27
splines, 25-27
Spy magazine, 58
Stacker, xvi
Star Trek—Deep Space 9 television series, 11
Star Trek VI: The Undiscovered Country, 10
STARS.GIF, 143
STARS.TGA, 129
Super VGA graphics mode, 72
Superman: the Movie, 139
SuperStor, xvi
SuperVGA graphics mode, xvii
SVHS connector, 66

SWIRL.MSH, 146
switches
    DMorf, 71-73
    DTA, 94-109
    FLISPEED, 109
    Trilobyte Play, 111
symmetric morphs, 61-64

T

task switching in Windows
    limitations with SuperVGA, xvii
television images
    capturing, 40-42
    creating, 65-66
television standards, 42
Tempra Turbo Animator, 91
Terminator 2: Judgment Day, 6, 10, 153
TEST.MSH, 71
text editor, 88, 93
texture
    transforming, 126-127
TGA file format, 22, 29, 42, 48, 56, 87-88
Thief of Baghdad, 149
Thriller video, 12, 128
tools reference
    DMorf, 70-90
    DTA, 90-109
    FLISPEED, 109-110
    Trilobyte Play, 110-111
transparency, 48-53
Trilobyte Play
    changing lunimence, 111
    changing speed of animation, 36
    command-line switches
        Changing Speed (-s), 111
        Looping (-l), 111
    displaying flics, 31
    installing, xiii-xviii
    memory requirements, xv, 111
    quitting, 31, 36
    registration, 110
    running under
    OS/2, xviii
        Windows, xvii
    smooth animation with, 36

starting, 110
    viewing flic animation files, 31
Truevision Targa+ graphics board, 65
tutorial
    creating control meshes, 22-29
    generating smooth animation, 34-36
    overview, 19
    quitting DMorf, 29
    refining control meshes, 31-34
    selecting pictures to morph, 20-21
    starting DMorf, 21-22
    testing morphs, 29-31
    viewing final morph, 36
Tyrannosaurus Rex morph, 4, 133-135

U

Ugly Duckling, 8
UNOCAL commercial, 13

V

vampires, 8
VCRs, 40, 65-66
vertical coordinates, 90
VESA 256-color resolution, 72
VGA monitors, 85-86, 98
video
    creating from morphs, 65-66
    hardware requirements, xiv
video digitizers, 20, 40-42, 54
video equipment
    connecting to computer, 40-42
video output, 65-66
VideoSpigot for Windows, 42
viewer programs. *see* Trilobyte Play
Vinton, Will, 43
Vivid ray tracer, 43, 54, 94
Volkswagen bug morph, 130-133

W

WARP
    in filenames, 87
Warp mode, 83
warping effects, 13-15, 22, 57-60

WATCH.BAT, 141-142
WATCH.FLI, 142
WAVE.MSH, 153
Wegner, Tim, 43, 99
Wells, Drew, 43
werewolf morph, 128-130
werewolves, 8
Willow, 9-10, 120-121
Windows, xvi-xvii, 21
Windows graphics file format, 94
WinImages:Morph, 70, 84
Wolf Man, 8, 128

X

XMS memory. *see* extended (XMS) memory

Y

You Can Call Me Ray BBS, 44
Young, Chris, 43

Z

Zeus, 7
ZIP file format, 94
Zoom mode, 50-53

Books have a substantial influence on the destruction of the forests of the Earth. For example, it takes 17 trees to produce one ton of paper. A first printing of 30,000 copies of a typical 480-page book consumes 108,000 pounds of paper which will require 918 trees!

Waite Group Press™ is against the clear-cutting of forests and supports reforestation of the Pacific Northwest of the United States and Canada, where most of this paper comes from. As a publisher with several hundred thousand books sold each year, we feel an obligation to give back to the planet. We will therefore support and contribute a percentage of our proceeds to organizations which seek to preserve the forests of planet Earth.

MAKING MOVIES ON YOUR PC

David Mason and Alexander Enzman

Flex your imagination and direct animated movies! You'll find everything you need to create fantastic rotating television logos, MTV-style action-clips, eye-boggling flybys and walkthroughs, or just about any movie effect you can dream up. The disks include the POLYRAY ray tracer for creating photorealistic images, and DTA, Dave's TGA Animator, the standard for converting ray-traced images to FLI movies. You'll also get ready-to-run example movies and explanations. No need to draw precise locations of objects and shadows—the included programs make realistic animation a snap; programming skills aren't required.

ISBN 1-878739-41-7, 200 pages, 2-5.25" disks, $34.95
Available now

VIRTUAL REALITY CREATIONS

Bernie Roehl, Dave Stampe, John Eagan

Walk, jump, fly, bound, or beam through virtual worlds, exploring them from your mouse or keyboard. With the included REND386 software and special Fresnel 3-D glasses, it's easy to build machine simulations, molecular models, video game environments, and much more. REND386 runs on any 386 or 486 system with a VGA adapter. No special VR hardware is required but many peripherals are supported. You'll find details on connecting special LCD glasses to view environments in 3-D, as well as instructions for making gloves that allow you to reach out and manipulate your creations.

ISBN: 1-878739-39-5, 300 pages, 1-5.25" disk and Fresnel viewers, $34.95
Available now

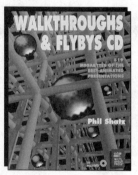

WALKTHROUGHS AND FLYBYS CD

Phil Shatz

Fly around buildings before they exist, tour the inner workings of imaginary machines, and play electronic music while watching the motion of atoms. Welcome to the world of animated PC demos, a new area of technology and design that relies on high-powered PCs, an assortment of graphics animation software, a Sound Blaster board, and some special tricks. The *Walkthroughs and Flybys CD* presents breathtaking computer animation and music including over 300 megabytes of Autodesk 3-D studio movies.

ISBN: 1-878739-40-9, 128 pages, 1-CD-ROM, $29.95
Available now

Send for our unique catalog to get more information about these books, as well as our outstanding and award-winning titles, including:

Master C: Let the PC Teach You C and **Master C++: Let the PC Teach You Object-Oriented Programming:** Both book/disk software packages turn your computer into an infinitely patient C and C++ professor.

Sound Effects Playhouse: An easy-to-use, hands on workshop for creating, editing and playing sounds under DOS and Windows. Includes 5MB of digitized sound files and utilities.

PDA PLayhouse: Test drive the office of the future with this guide. Mac and PC simulations of the Apple Newton, Sharp Wizard and AT&T EO, and others are included.

Artificial Life Lab: Cyberpunk pioneer Rudy Rucker leads you on an interactive examination of a-life programming. Using the included Windows program Boppers, you'll design and populate your own world. Includes 3D glasses.

Fractals for Windows: Create new fractals and control over 85 different fractal types with a zoom box, menus, and a mouse! Comes with WINFRACT, a powerful Windows version of FRACTINT for DOS, this package is faster than lightning at computing mind-bending fractals.

Virtual Reality Playhouse: Jack-in to the world of Virtual Reality with this playful book/disk package. Eight demos with VR simulations let you create your own personal digital dimension.

Nanotechnology Playhouse: This book and disk set is an accessible introduction to nanotechnology (the science of making devices, materials, objects of all kinds, one atom at a time). It includes multimedia demos to give you a taste of tomorrow.

Artificial Life Playhouse: Turn your PC into an experimenter's lab to find out more about this exciting new area of scientific exploration. Eight demo programs are included.

This is a legal agreement between you, the end user and purchaser, and The Waite Group®, Inc., and the authors of the programs contained in the disk. By opening the sealed disk package, you are agreeing to be bound by the terms of this Agreement. If you do not agree with the terms of this Agreement, promptly return the unopened disk package and the accompanying items (including the related book and other written material) to the place you obtained them for a refund.

SOFTWARE LICENSE

1. The Waite Group, Inc. grants you the right to use one copy of the enclosed software programs (the programs) on a single computer system (whether a single CPU, part of a licensed network, or a terminal connected to a single CPU). Each concurrent user of the program must have exclusive use of the related Waite Group, Inc. written materials.

2. The program, including the copyrights in each program, is owned by the respective author and the copyright in the entire work is owned by The Waite Group, Inc. and they are therefore protected under the copyright laws of the United States and other nations, under international treaties. You may make only one copy of the disk containing the programs exclusively for backup or archival purposes, or you may transfer the programs to one hard disk drive, using the original for backup or archival purposes. You may make no other copies of the programs, and you may make no copies of all or any part of the related Waite Group, Inc. written materials.

3. You may not rent or lease the programs, but you may transfer ownership of the programs and related written materials (including any and all updates and earlier versions) if you keep no copies of either, and if you make sure the transferee agrees to the terms of this license.

4. You may not decompile, reverse engineer, disassemble, copy, create a derivative work, or otherwise use the programs except as stated in this Agreement.

GOVERNING LAW

This Agreement is governed by the laws of the State of California.

SOFTWARE LICENSE AGREEMENT

SATISFACTION REPORT CARD

Please fill out this card if you wish to know of future updates to
Morphing On Your PC, or to receive our catalog.

WAITE GROUP PRESS™

Company Name: _____

Division/Department: _____ Mail Stop: _____

Last Name: _____ First Name: _____ Middle Initial: _____

Street Address: _____

City: _____ State: _____ Zip: _____

Daytime telephone: (   ) _____

Date product was acquired: Month _____ Day _____ Year _____ Your Occupation: _____

Overall, how would you rate *Morphing On Your PC*?
- ☐ Excellent ☐ Very Good ☐ Good
- ☐ Fair ☐ Below Average ☐ Poor

What did you like MOST about this book? _____
_____

What did you like LEAST about this book? _____
_____
_____

Please describe any problems you may have encountered with installing or using the programs: _____
_____

How did you use this book (problem-solver, tutorial, reference...)?
_____

What is your level of computer expertise?
- ☐ New ☐ Dabbler ☐ Hacker
- ☐ Power User ☐ Programmer ☐ Experienced Professional

What computer languages are you familiar with? _____
_____

Please describe your computer hardware:
Computer _____ Hard disk _____
5.25" disk drives _____ 3.5" disk drives _____
Video card _____ Monitor _____
Sound Board _____ CD ROM _____
Printer _____ Peripherals _____

Where did you buy this book?
- ☐ Bookstore (name): _____
- ☐ Discount store (name): _____
- ☐ Computer store (name): _____
- ☐ Catalog (name): _____
- ☐ Direct from WGP ☐ Other _____

What price did you pay for this book? _____

What influenced your purchase of this book?
- ☐ Recommendation ☐ Advertisement
- ☐ Magazine review ☐ Store display
- ☐ Mailing ☐ Book's format
- ☐ Reputation of Waite Group Press ☐ Other

How many computer books do you buy each year? _____

How many other Waite Group books do you own? _____

What is your favorite Waite Group book? _____
_____

Is there any program or subject you would like to see Waite Group Press cover in a similar approach? _____
_____
_____

Additional comments? _____
_____
_____

☐ **Check here for a free Waite Group catalog**

Morphing On Your PC

Waite Group Press, Inc.
Attention: *Morphing On Your PC*
200 Tamal Plaza
Corte Madera, CA 94925

-- **FOLD HERE** --